Success and Failure in Professional Education: Assessing the Evidence

Irene Ilott

Group Head of Research and Development,
College of Occupational Therapists, London, UK

and

Roger Murphy

Director of Research, School of Education,
University of Nottingham, UK

Whurr Publishers
London

© 1999 Whurr Publishers Ltd
First published 1999 by
Whurr Publishers Ltd
19b Compton Terrace
London N1 2UN

British Library Cataloguing-in-Publication Data
A catalogue record for this book is available from the British Library.

ISBN 1 86156 070 2

Printed and bound in Great Britain by Athenæum Press Ltd, Gateshead, Tyne & Wear.

WY
18.8
ILO

T   low.

Contents

Chapter 4

Chapter 5

Chapter 6

Chapter 7

Appendix 1

Foreword

The privilege and responsibility of self-regulation is one of the characteristics of a profession. The following extract from the Government's White Paper, *The New NHS – Modern, Dependable* (December 1997), emphasises the importance attached to professional self-regulation of the medical profession.

> The Government will continue to look to individual health professionals to be responsible for the quality of their own clinical practice. Professional self-regulation must remain an essential element in the delivery of quality patient services. It is crucial that the professional standards developed nationally continue to be responsive to changing service needs and to legitimate public expectations. The Government will continue to work with the professions, the NHS and patient representative groups to strengthen the existing systems of professional self-regulation by ensuring that they are open, responsive and publicly accountable.

The primary purpose of self-regulation is to protect the public from practitioners who are deficient in knowledge, skills, attitude and conduct. Professions feel strongly that only their members have the necessary insight to judge other members. If, however, professions wish to continue to self-regulate and enjoy the trust and respect of patients, then it is essential that each profession embraces the challenge of failure.

The General Medical Council (GMC), the statutory body responsible for regulating the medical profession, has as its motto '*Protecting patients, guiding doctors*' and, in May 1996, stated:

> We are committed to a system of medical regulation which is open and accountable; and to developing procedures and processes that are effective, fair, objective, transparent and free from discrimination.

Irene Ilott and Roger Murphy's timely book *Success and Failure in Professional Education: Assessing the Evidence* attempts to demystify failure for professionals and tackle this taboo subject in an erudite manner with many examples drawn from various professions.

The introductory chapter emphasizes that failure is a necessity and is part of life. To fail in a profession is not to fail as a whole person and may be a catalyst for change. How often has a trainee felt a weight of responsibility lifted from his shoulders? Failure can be positive if handled positively.

Selection for professions is not foolproof. Therefore the willingness of those in charge of training to fail students is essential to protect society. Each profession must develop strategies for failure to facilitate the gatekeeper role which is essential to ensure the quality of future practice and protect vulnerable service users. The strategy should be transparent, fair and free from discrimination. Failure is essential for the well-being of members of professions, since working with incompetent colleagues is a major source of stress and often creates ethical dilemmas. The General Medical Council has introduced performance procedures and thus has given 'permission' to doctors to judge colleagues' performance and if found deficient or incompetent, to report these individuals to the GMC.

But what is professional competence and what is incompetence?

Both remain 'elusive concepts' upon which the authors endeavour to shed some light. The behaviourist and attributional approaches are rejected in favour of the integrated approach which acknowledges the importance of context, professional judgement, reasoning and ethics. This approach means that judgement of attitudes and conduct or behaviour assumes as much importance as skills. Suddenly, the authors have helped illuminate a grey area for professions and given a framework around which professional competence may be judged. This competence includes professional behaviour towards colleagues and weaves together knowledge, skills (clinical and non-clinical), attitudes and conduct, including honesty and integrity. All are essential attributes for the practising professional.

Professional competence should include the skills necessary to fail students, trainees and colleagues. Failure to fail is 'professional cowardice' and could itself be considered a form of 'educational malpractice'. The GMC and the Government would feel that this is a basic tenet of continuation of self-regulation. Thus, the doctor who fails to fail another's performance, could himself/herself be reported to the GMC.

Professions do not stand still. Neither do the expectations of the society which they serve. Behaviour and conduct which was acceptable a decade ago may now be unacceptable, e.g. the changes in equal opportunities. Consequently each profession requires to continually re-evaluate the constituents of integrated competence. The strategy for failure needs to be continually re-assessed.

This book should be read by all professionals, especially those with responsibility for training. The attitudes of professions towards failure are explored and reassurance is given that increased accountability need not necessarily challenge personal or professional autonomy.

Professions who are seen to accept the challenge of failure will continue to self-regulate, enjoy autonomy and bask in the trust of their 'clients' – the latter so essential for professional well-being.

Rosemary Macdonald, PhD, FRCA.
August 1998

Preface

Background

While there is a wealth of literature about assessment there is very little about the feelings, thoughts and behaviour associated with failing students. The word and deed tend to be avoided via anonymous pass lists in higher education or statements of 'not yet competent' with permission for endless repeats in National Vocational Qualifications. This may constitute denial thus adding to concerns about assessment standards in academic and work-based settings. The problems are exacerbated when assessment underpins registration as competent to practise a profession. This can occur in any vocational course designed to prepare practitioners to work with the public – or service users – whether patients, pupils, or clients – who place their faith in the skill, knowledge and ethical behaviour of the professional. Although diverse in terms of content and context all professional practice is based upon trust. Any abuse of the power and privilege conferred by a professional relationship is not acceptable. Professions, whether corporate bodies or individual practitioners have a duty to protect the public from unsafe, incompetent and unscrupulous colleagues. This is because the collective responsibility of professional and statutory bodies is vested in individual assessors.

The study

Much of the material for this book is drawn from Irene Ilott's PhD research into the staff perspective on the process of assigning a fail grade in occupational therapy conducted between 1989 and 1993. A qualitative research design was used to explore, to understand and explain the multiple interpretations of this emotive topic. The study involved a literature review, questionnaire surveys and in-depth interviews. The principal method was focused interviews with 30 occupational therapy educators to compare the perspective of managers, lecturers, work-placement organisers and work-based supervisors. The book is peppered with many quotations derived from the interviews to illustrate and provide real-life examples. The two questionnaire surveys provided supplementary information. On the first survey 64 per cent (n=72) trained, experienced work-based assessors ranked 'failing a student' as their toughest responsibility (Ilott, 1996). The second postal survey comprised immediate and follow-up (at three and twelve months) evaluations of five, one day 'failure workshops' attended by 101 work-based assessors. The evaluations highlighted the importance of an assessors' affective response, reinforced effective supervisory strategies and the obligation to act as a gatekeeper of professional standards (Ilott, 1995).

Each component of the study highlighted how challenging pass–fail decisions are for assessors. Judging 'competence to practise' is a formidable responsibility. The difficulties associated with failing proved to be common, almost universal in that they crossed professions and sectors such as medicine, teaching and social work. This is why the book adopts a broad approach to professional education. However, the book essentially emerged from a study of one profession – occupational therapy – which crosses the boundaries of health, social care and education. Readers are invited to extrapolate from the examples to their own situation.

The book

Experienced or inexperienced assessors working in academic establishments or work settings are the target audience. The aim is to demystify fail scenarios, to explain the dilemmas which can sabotage judgements, to promote rigor and best assessment practise but, most importantly, to give assessors permission to fulfil their role as 'guardians of standards'. The principles apply to pre- and post-registration students. This encompasses those seeking entry to or continuance within a profession. The latter may be part of a mandatory mechanism for assuring continued competence, a voluntary scheme for continued professional development, or to gain access to a speciality. While no qualification or examination can guarantee safe, competent and ethical conduct there remains a duty to be alert and to act, rather than ignore instances when students or staff do not attain or maintain acceptable standards.

This is the message of the whole book, but particularly Chapters 1 and 2. The first chapter reviews the taboo status of failing and failure, especially the negative stereotypes due to the association between failure on a task and as a person. A 'terror of errors' in a 'blame culture' would seem to exacerbate the problem. Chapter 2 sets the background for clear threshold standards in vocational programmes where there is co-terminosity of academic award and registration with a statutory or professional body to work with the public. The next two chapters describe the reasons why assigning a fail grade is so difficult. Chapter 3 presents a multi-faceted model to disentangle the subtle, interacting individual, institutional and external factors which influence examiners when making judgements at the margins of competence. Chapter 4 highlights the fears and feelings which may sabotage or confirm the decision-making process for the teacher-as-judge. Good assessment practices provide the foundation for dealing with the added difficulties when dealing with borderline students. These are summarised in Chapter 5. In Chapter 6 they are applied throughout the assessment cycle of eliciting, interpreting and acting on the evidence. This detailed chapter uses the legal metaphor of making judgements 'on the balance of probabilities' or 'beyond reasonable doubt' to ensure justice and 'due process' through respecting the rights and responsibilities of all concerned. The final chapter is an executive summary of the whole book. It contains a risk management approach with recommendations for change to reduce the number of 'horror stories' about the abuse of vulnerable service users. This long-term perspective is a key mediating factor. It is needed to counter the immediate work stress of assigning a fail grade and the utilitarian climate of performance indicators or financial viability.

Acknowledgements

Irene Illot's PhD research was supervised by Dr Eric Hall of the Faculty of Education at the University of Nottingham. The study was supported by the Constance Owen Trust, Liverpool College of Occupational Therapy and colleagues at the Derby School of Occupational Therapy, especially Joan Kenyon and Vivian Wallace. It depended upon the co-operation of all the academic and work-based assessors who generously shared their experiences. The contribution of Marjorie Allen, Donald Bligh and David Ilott in ensuring the transformation of the research into a book is acknowledged.

Chapter 1
Failure: an easily avoided word and deed

Introduction

Although there is much discussion of the need for rigorous standards in courses designed to prepare people to become professionally qualified, the topic of failure on such courses seems to be neglected. Tutors often avoid talking about failure, preferring to use politically correct euphemisms such as 'non-attainment' or refer to 'at risk' students. It is as if failure and failing are taboo topics. While there is more written about other taboo subjects, such as sex, religion and death, the literature dealing with failure is surprisingly sparse. This book aims to redress this imbalance by focusing upon the assessors' perspective when making pass–fail judgements in professional education.

The education and training literature tends to stress the need to diagnose difficulties in student learning and then suggest remediation and support strategies. This approach is perhaps more comfortable because it implies that something can be done, the problem can be resolved. There is however, in our view, a need to confront the fact that not all students will, can or should succeed. Some students may, for a wide variety of reasons, be unsuitable for the profession they wish to join. Professional education programmes must have exit routes for those who fail to achieve the threshold standard of knowledge, competence and conduct. Such decisions are difficult. They can be highly stressful both for students and for their tutors, assessors and external examiners. Professional education can create a more intense, 'high stakes' assessment situation than is experienced in other branches of higher education. All those involved are usually painfully aware of how much is at stake, yet assessment proced-ures are not foolproof. Judgements about professional competence are made with varying degrees of skill and confidence. We hope by providing an evidence-based, practical guide, this book will help academic and work-based assessors make the better decisions informed by the latest research and thinking on this topic.

Unless it is possible to fail then it is unlikely that a course can guarantee minimum professional standards. Most staff do not relish the task of conveying 'bad news', especially when a fail grade requires a student to withdraw from professional training. This can be a particularly shattering blow for students who are mature entrants as it may signal an abrupt end to their career aspirations. Clearly it is easy for such circumstances and consequences to interfere with the quality of decision making, especially at the margins of 'competence to practise'.

This book explores the complexity of fail scenarios in professional education so that educators may be encouraged to confront and challenge the various taboos. Failing is a natural part of life and learning. It is unrealistic to expect success in everything all the time. We learn from mistakes, from trying and failing, by trial and error. Failure may be a catalyst for a change of direction or approach. It is a stimulus for new and different learning. It can be used to very good effect within diagnostic and formative assessment schemes to encourage further learning and development in an informed, well-focused way. This positive approach is epitomised by Dorothy Crowfoot Hodgkin, the only British woman to win a Nobel prize for science. In response to a journalist listing her achievements in determining the structure of penicillin, vitamin B12 and insulin, she interrupted, 'You ought to realise that for 90 per cent of my life I'm dealing with failure, and occasionally I have a success' (Wojtas, 1995).

Failing an academic assignment or work placement may trigger all sorts of actions and responses, but it may be only failure on a task and does not necessarily imply failure of the whole educational programme or the people involved. Claxton (1984) describes the association of 'having failed, the guilty burden of not being "good enough" – a flawed person'. This debilitating association between self-image and professional competence must be severed. It can damage the self-esteem of the student and the assessor, and fears stemming from it can impair judgements and thus threaten threshold standards in professional education.

Historically, standards were guarded more by rigorous selection procedures at the point of admission to professional education rather than at the point of qualification. Recent initiatives to open access to higher education to traditionally under-represented groups has placed much more emphasis on exit standards, learning outcomes and benchmarking information. Such threshold standards need to be explicit and robust. They are a particularly important part of the present when they provide the reference level or criteria for failure to help staff implement exit procedures.

This book is based upon the premise that it is as wrong to fail someone who should pass, as to pass someone who should fail. Yet examiners in academic and work settings often appear to be much more concerned to avoid the former than the latter. Failure in such situations can be denied by giving the 'benefit of the doubt' and allowing students to 'just pass'. Failure in professional education is nevertheless a crucial topic which deserves to be explored and uncovered so that it can come to be seen as a healthy aspect of such courses. If it is indeed a taboo topic then there is an urgent need to break the taboo and promote discussion. Like other taboos much damage can result from a lack of openness about things that are hugely significant in the lives of individuals.

A fail grade is also a unidimensional symbol with multidimensional meanings (Pollio, Humphreys and Milton, 1989). The meanings ascribed by those responsible for judging 'competence to practise' are explored throughout the book. Although failure 'affects comparatively few, it dramatically affects those few' (Howard, 1979). It is a potentially 'debilitating, emotionally draining experience' (Symanski, 1991). This is why it is important to understand so that assessors may optimise their decision making and reduce the incidence of 'failure to fail' (Lankshear, 1990).

Definitions and meanings

The Concise Oxford Dictionary (1991) defines failure as 'lack of success ... an unsuccessful person, thing, or attempt, non-performance. Failing, a fault or shortcoming, a weakness especially in character. Failed, unsuccessful, not good enough, weak, deficient, broken down. Fail, not succeed (failed in persuading, failed to qualify, tried but failed)... rejected as a candidate, be unable to, choose not to, disappoint, let down.' The definition is full of negative associations and stereotypes, even though failure is a natural part of life and learning. For this reason, the definition used in this book is *the non-achievement of a specific task* or *the non-attainment of a prescribed standard.* This definition separates failure on a task from failure in any wider sense, for example, 'as a person'.

Yet words are more complex than dictionary definitions. They contain many meanings. Pollio, Eison and Milton, (1998), Pollio et al., (1989), and Pollio, Humphreys and Eison (1991), investigated the meaning of college grades for students and parents in America. They concluded that multidimensional meanings were being assigned to unidimensional symbols. This means different students valued the same grade differently. Meaning is denotative and connotative. Denotation is the operational definition. It refers to the object designated by a symbol or the procedure by which the symbol is defined. For example, it refers to the way in which examiners use formal and informal assessment methods to decide upon a grade. In contrast, connotation refers to the broader implications – the emotional tone and social value – suggested by the symbol.

The connotative meaning comprises three components, as follows:

Trait meaning – is the way in which students, staff, parents and employers use grades to describe aspects of student personality, particularly intelligence, personal adjustment and the ability to work in a system. Grades, as a reflection of potential and to predict future life success, are an important part of judging borderline students (see Chapter 2).

Social meaning – provides others with information about the student. It is presumed to motivate and prepare the students for their future life, to reflect academic and teaching standards and also as a way of pleasing parents. The social meaning of grades is apparent in the symbolic power of league tables and concern about 'grade inflation'.

Personal grade evaluation – is the meaning of the grade for individual students. It contains their reactions and values. This is influenced by the relevance, satisfaction, importance and effort associated with obtaining the grade. Personal meaning explains the variation in student reaction including unexpected responses such as equanimity (Wilson, 1972). It is important to elicit and understand the student's frame of reference. The assessor should not presume other meanings or impose their meaning.

The significance of a 'fail' grade can be influenced by invidious comparison with others who have passed or failed. It is another reason why failure is feared. Comparisons may be formal or informal. Individual and group results are often subjected to detailed analyses – often giving them far greater significance than is warranted. Politicians and journalists love to detect and comment upon trends in assessment results, either to proclaim that standards of education are falling, or if the results are getting better to conclude that the assessment standards are getting easier (Murphy, 1996). We now live in an age of league tables and assessment results in every phrase of education. They are used to create simple tables which regularly imply much more meaning than is justified (Murphy, 1997). Such league tables are intended to represent statements about standards in education. They are intended to enhance openness, transparency and accountability through appraisal of facilities and results. Sadly they frequently tend to misinform the very people they are supposed to inform. The apparently simple statistics, for example of a school's examination results, can only be interpreted sensibly in relation to a much more detailed knowledge of the school, its intake of pupils and facilities.

In work-based settings assessors tend to use experience, observation and anecdote as the basis for comparing student performance rather than statistical evidence. Assessments tend to be ideographic. This means individuals are measured against criterion-referenced standards as competent or not yet competent. This may apply to a particular task, or key personal transferable skills, or be based upon global judgements of competence related to stage of training. Although failure is less comparative it can seem more personal. 'It is about the student as an individual because it relates to interpersonal skills' (work-based assessor).

Definitions are complicated by multiple meanings. Fail, a simple four-letter word, is subject to different interpretations depending upon personal perceptions, meanings and comparisons. It is these ramifications which make failure – defined here as the non-achievement of a specific task or the non-attainment of a prescribed standard – so difficult.

Avoidance of the 'f' word

Failure, or the likelihood of a student failing, are often avoided through the use of softer labels or metaphors. These include non-attainment, non-achievement and 'at risk'. Euphemisms reflect the context, culture, educational philosophy and concept of learning. Yet clear language helps to convey the right message. Plewis (1991) advocates the abandonment of the ambiguous term 'under-achievement' to reduce the conceptual and operational confusion which hinders educational research. During an investigation into beliefs and thoughts about 'at risk' students, Koehler (1988) described teachers' frustration with themselves and the school system, yet he observed that 'neither teacher used the words failure or failing with respect to any of their students at any point in the long interviews'.

Such avoidance has been reported from kindergarten to doctoral students. Yet more politically correct words still convey the same meaning even for the youngest students. Kindergarten children subject to the American system of retention recognised the reality of 'flunking the grade'. They reported being teased and feeling a sense of failure. Their teachers did not tell them they would be retaking the year – parents gave the bad news (Shepard and Smith, 1989). There is a similar avoidance in the United Kingdom where school examination grades, for example at GCSE level, are defined in terms of D and E. These are equivalent to the former fail grade at 'O' level. Students receive an 'unclassified' grade as opposed to being failed. This is an example of grading criteria not using the term. On other assessment schemes failure may not even be an option. For example, the National Council for Vocational Qualifications set two outcomes – competent and not yet competent. Resits are permitted until competence is achieved. Avoidance occurs in universities too, for example when a degree programme uses a grading system with the letters A to F accompanied by descriptors which define the bottom categories (E–F) as 'unsuccessful' and 'unacceptable'. This is an institutionally sanctioned and sanitised avoidance mechanism. However, the situation is changing. Examination Boards in some institutions are now directed to use 'fail' rather than 'unsuccessful' when notifying students of their results. Unambiguous language is necessary to protect the institution from student appeals.

Individual assessors may also be reluctant in such situations to say what they are thinking. The danger of semantic avoidance is passing a student who should fail. Euphemisms may protect the student's (and examiner's) self-esteem. 'We did not want to upset them, so they feel worthless' (work-based supervisor). There is a tendency to be too constructive: 'you only need to do this' to 'hedge with words like unsatisfactory' rather than be candid and direct. A supervisor commented, 'I do not like being judgemental. It is difficult to face up to the situation of a failing student.'

Yet students need (and expect) honest, unambiguous feedback. A fail grade should not come as a surprise in a good programme of professional education. If this happens the student has been deprived of 'due process'. They have been treated unfairly through lack of information and the opportunity to improve. A study into the assessment of clinical progress of student nurses revealed 95 per cent favoured receiving 'justified adverse comments' on their performance (Bradley, 1990). Assessors have a duty to review progress, identify problems and improvements needed, suggest alternative strategies and monitor change towards an agreed goal. Written statements may have more impact, particularly for those who do not wish to hear the word or who lack insight. A work-based organiser observed a 'fail written in pencil or pen can be rubbed out' whereas if typed, it was a 'straight communication'. The student 'could not cling to hope as if they have not heard the term'. The importance of the written word was noted in Gleason's study (1984): 'The students need something more concrete than words to guide them toward satisfactory grade acquisition' (p. 218). When the meeting was supported by a grade adjustment plan – a visual record charting problems and action – negotiated with the student and monitored through periodic reviews, 70 per cent improved their grades. Again, in the context of schools, Black and Wiliam (1998) have shown what a powerful force for improvement good, honest and clear formative assessment can be to motivate students to improve their learning.

When assessors do assign a fail grade their judgement may of course be challenged by colleagues and their educational establishment. There may be pressure to pass. A work-based assessor described 'being condemned by the school because they will see the student's failure as our fault'. Such pressure has been reported by teachers (Norcross, 1991), health visitors, general practitioners and social workers (Green, 1991), nurses (Symanski, 1991), occupational therapists (Ilott, 1993) and midwives (Fraser, Murphy and Worth-Butler, 1997). Green (1991), in a study of undergraduate and postgraduate professional training, describes the strength of negative feelings, the lack of support from colleagues, managers and lecturing staff when making the decision, with some practice teachers even experiencing considerable pressure to pass a student when it was against their professional judgement.

Considering how easy it is to avoid – as a word and deed – it is unsurprising there are so few fails which result in the termination of a training programme. It is a difficult and rare event. This book is intended to explore this phenomenon, to help assessors confront the taboo and to make good judgements.

Incidence and pattern of fails

Failure can be a rare event in some areas of professional education. Fails, like the success of first class honours degrees, are the extremes of a distribution curve of results. Although attrition, wastage or drop-out rates give some indication of the frequency of fails, they can be misleading. Students leave higher education for a range of voluntary as well as involuntary reasons. This section introduces the incidence and pattern of fails. Unsurprisingly, little has been written about this topic. We will also look at the impact of factors such as league tables and funding mechanisms which can be driven by output statistics. These are external factors which can exert an influence on individuals and institutions when they are making decisions about threshold standards. They also contribute to a growing unease about grade inflation and the gradual lowering of certain educational standards.

The pattern of fail grades is considered in the context of attrition statistics. This is to assist assessors and reassure students who are often plagued by a fear of failure. The figures should be seen as indicating trends rather than being definitive. This is because of the variation in assessment regulations for courses and between higher education institutions. The diversity of regulations for credit accumulation and modular schemes adds to this complexity.

Attrition rates, reasons and consequences

Non-completion rates in British higher education have fluctuated between 14 and 18 per cent over the past ten years. The Survey of Student Financial Support 1995, a report commissioned by the Committee of Vice Chancellors and Principals, notes drop-out rates are somewhat higher than the growth rate in student numbers. There was a 20 per cent (n=21,000) increase in the number due to examination failure in 1995 in comparison with 1994. However, it should be noted that there are even higher rates of non-completion in other countries. For example, the Organisation for Economic Cooperation and Development's 'Education at a Glance 1997' and 'Education Policy Analysis 1997' indicate drop out rates in higher education of up to 64 per cent in Italy and 34 per cent in Germany. A study reported in the *Times Higher Education Supplement* (Cornwell, 1997) estimated that half of doctoral students in the United States do not complete their studies and that this pattern had persisted over 'the past few decades'.

Attrition rates for health care professions are also variable. The following examples illustrate the variation. There was a 9.5 per cent attrition rate for a New Zealand medical school over a 25 year period

(Collins and White, 1993). Different attrition rates have been reported for nurse assessments. Dopson (1987) reported a 7 per cent fail rate on the final national examination in Scotland while Harvey and Vaughan (1990) expressed concern about the 35 per cent wastage rate in any given cohort in the United Kingdom. The National Council licensing examination for Registered Nurses in America is constructed to achieve a failure rate of 10 per cent (Dell and Valine, 1990) while the membership examination for the Royal College of Physicians (UK) has a fixed pass rate of 30 per cent.

Non-completion rates are complicated and notoriously difficult to interpret. This is related to the many definitions, causes, costs and consequences of non-completion. Such definitions need to accommodate the range of voluntary and involuntary reasons for departure (Mashaba and Mhlongo, 1995). Students may choose to leave higher education to take advantage of better opportunities, change direction or because they obtain employment. Circumstances may force the discontinuation of studies. These include personal problems and financial reasons – the cost of living and studying, difficulties with accommodation and transport – as well as failing to meet the required standards. Another reason for attrition is discontent with the course. Academic failure may be aggravated by part-time work, debt, family disruption or ill-health for example. At postgraduate level, the social and financial structures which integrate or exclude doctoral students from the university are important factors. Non-completion can be due to a complex combination of reasons.

The costs and benefits of non-completion are equally complicated. Benefits are possible. A study by Wilson (1972) revealed three reactions to failure amongst first year arts and sciences students at a Scottish university. These were equanimity, resentment or guilt. Equanimity was expressed by students who were dissatisfied with university life, were pleased to leave an 'uncongenial atmosphere' and who took subjects which bored them. The costs mirror an ambivalent attitude toward drop-out rates. A moderate one may be perceived as healthy, indicating intellectual rigour and respect for maintaining minimum standards. However, concern rises in proportion to the number of withdrawals. The temptation to apportion blame (especially 'poor teachers') and accept simplistic explanations mask complex scenarios. Entry criteria are an obvious causal factor for attrition. Britain's historically low non-completion rates were due to the high, pre-entry requirements for higher education. The policy to increase access for a broader and larger section of the community has created a different context. It could be argued that increasing the intake and maintaining exit standards means that more students should fail. Westcott (1995) provides a counter argument. She is concerned that the open door is becoming a revolving door for non-traditional students because they are 'frequently misinformed, under-motivated and ill-prepared for the experience of higher education' (p. 14).

The costs of attrition are borne by individuals and institutions in a variety of ways. The literature recommends 'at risk' students be identified early, offered support (academic and pastoral) to 'help mitigate the demoralisation, depression and decline in motivation' (Croen, Reichgott and Spencer, 1991, p. 487) associated with fails. Such institutional strategies to minimise attrition are not just for altruistic motives. Loss of fee income is an even more important motivating factor, especially with the threat of output-related funding. Initially, assisting 'at risk' students to succeed was based upon ethical concerns to 'maximise human resources'. It has now become a 'matter of institutional survival' (Gupta, 1991). This is for a variety of reasons. Demographic changes have led to increasing competition for national and international students. Quantitative outputs or performance indicators promoted via league tables are public statements which influence policymakers, prospective students and funding agencies. Furthermore output-related funding can be seen as an equivalent to payment by results. This method of funding National Vocational Qualifications was criticised by the National Institute for Economic and Social Research in August 1995. It is open to abuse and can thus devalue the qualification. Results may not be trusted when payment depends on outcomes or penalties are imposed for drop-out. All these factors contribute to an impression that institutions have a vested interest in ensuring all pass even though selection processes are notoriously fallible.

There are also many emotional costs. Fortunately, the most extreme, sad consequence – suicide – is rare (Tytler, 1995). The student may experience a 'wounded self-image' from feeling a failure (Mashaba and Mhlongo, 1995). This is likely to be even more pronounced for professionals pursuing further qualifications, especially if it stops career progression. For example, Adshead et al. (1984) describes failure in general practice examinations as a substantial set-back for self-esteem since it carries the implication that the doctor is unfit for this role. These costs can be shared by the students' family, the cohort and staff who may also experience loss when they see that their investment of personal time and energy does not help the student to achieve (Lengacher and Keller, 1990). Failing can generate a complex set of emotional reactions amongst all the stakeholders. These are explored in Chapter 4.

There are broader consequences of attrition. These can include the loss of a precious training place: a high price for professions in which there is a shortage of places and practitioners with a demand from service users. At a more distant level, the tax-payer or society can see a loss of return from their investment in education. In 1997 the Higher Education Funding Council estimated the actual cost of non-completion at £178 million.

The causes and costs of attrition provide the background to the frequency of fails as a reason for non-completion. However, there is one more rider. This is the importance of differentiating between a first and a final fail.

Differentiating between first and final fails

Most assessment regulations for higher education in the UK permit a first ever fail on a course of professional education to be retrieved. The student is allowed to resit the examination, resubmit a piece of course work or repeat a work placement. This gives extra learning time in which to prove competence. There are opportunities to practise, consolidate, gain confidence and achieve the required level for the stage of training. In exceptional circumstances a third attempt may be approved, with or without the stipulation of repeating the year, module or unit of assessment. A second fail usually results in withdrawal from the programme. This means the training is terminated. In some countries there is no limit on the number of retakes – this also applies to National Vocational Qualifications in the United Kingdom. For some post-qualifying qualifications, such as the examination for Membership of the Royal College of Physicians, five resits are permitted. Again this is a controversial area prompting some politicians to criticise modular A levels because they allow students too many opportunities to demonstrate their learning! This stance shows a limited understanding of the concept of exit standards and related approaches to mastery learning or competence-based education, for example.

Awarding a fail grade regardless of whether it is for the first time or not, seems to provoke the same distress, especially for work-based assessors. Yet the costs and consequences are very different. Unfamiliarity can add to the problem. Examiners lack preparation, experience and therefore confidence in failing. Where the reasons for non-completion are recorded, some general trends about the incidence of first or subsequent fails in different years emerge. Understanding these trends may reassure students too.

An example: wastage rates in occupational therapy

During the last two decades the non-completion rate in occupational therapy has been declining while the intake has been increasing – a different pattern from other higher education courses. For example, between 1967–1974 the attrition rate ranged from 20 per cent to 29 per cent (Stewart, 1980) and between 1975–1983 it ranged from 22 per cent to 13 per cent (Paterson, 1988). Since 1980 nine reasons for withdrawal have been collected. The categories of health, academic, clinical, wrong career choice, personal/domestic, immaturity, transferred, deferred and other are defined in Table 1.1. Only a single category is used for the national returns which means it is open to individual interpretation (Paterson, 1988). Academic failure defined as 'student unable to cope with the course, demonstrates inability to learn by failure on internal or professional assessment' was the most common reason (with the exception of wrong career choice in year one) during the time of the study (Ilott, 1993). The pattern is illustrated in Table 1.1

The number of non-completions was 80 (7.4%) in year one, 45 (5.1%) in year two and 17 (2%) in year three. The number of those failing for academic reasons peaked in year two. Only six students left due to clinical work meaning they were 'unable to function at the expected level, showed difficulty with relationships or demonstrated unsuitability to the profession in other ways'. These were split between the second and final year. This attrition rate is comparable with those collected by the Committee on Allied Health Education and Accreditation in America which monitors the annual, national intake and output data for 26 professions. For the academic year 1989–1990 there was a 4.4 per cent wastage rate for occupational therapy (Gupta, 1991).

This pattern obtained from national statistics mirrored the experience of academic and work-based assessors during 30 focused interviews. They reported that most academic failures occur in the first year with most work-based failures occurring in years two and three. This is an interesting difference. Academic staff seem more likely to award a fail grade early in the course whereas work-based assessors are more likely to do so later. Importantly, in both settings, half of those failing were successful at the second attempt – on the retake assessment. This can be seen to confirm the learning value of a first fail. It gives extra time and practice, and half of those given this further opportunity succeed the second time around.

In occupational therapy it seems that academic failure is a small but significant component of overall non-completion rates. However, this is undoubtedly influenced by another confounding variable. This is what Lankshear calls 'unprofessional cowardice...the failure to fail' (1990).

Failure to fail

The issue of whether some A level examinations and National Vocational Qualifications were too easy to pass attracted media attention during 1996. Only 5 of 5,341 candidates (i.e. 0.09%) were awarded a fail grade in the English and English Literature A level examinations administered by the Oxford and Cambridge School Examinations Board. The board was criticised for 'serious misconduct' because of the poor validity and reliability of these 'gold standard' qualifications (Baty, 1997). A similar pattern was reported in the very different context of work-based qualifications (level 2 and 3 NVQs) for engineering, construction and administration. On a postal survey, 38 per cent of 1,057 of those associated with these qualifications agreed with the question 'In the present assessment system, do you feel that many candidates pass who shouldn't?' The authors comment 'most astonishing are the higher figures of 41 per cent for internal verifiers and 48 per cent for external verifiers, suggesting that the greater their knowledge and experience of NVQ assessment, the more likely it is that assessors feel that wrong decisions are being made' (Eraut et al., 1996, p. 65).

Table 1.1 Patterns and reasons for non-completion amongst first, second and third year occupational therapy students between 1987–1990

Year	Total number in the cohort	Health	Academic	Clinical	Wrong career choice	Personal/domestic	Immaturity	Other	Total
1989–90 intake	1076	7	20	–	32	13	5	3	80 / 7%
1988–89 intake	881	1	24	3	10	4	2	1	45 / 5%
1987–88 intake	830	2	6	3	3	1	–	2	17 / 2%

Definitions

Health: Withdrawal of student on medical grounds, either physical or psychiatric. Prolonged ill health which prevents the student from completing the course and/or performing the duties as an occupational therapist.

Academic: Academically, student unable to cope with the course – demonstrates inability to learn by failure of internal or professional assessment.

Clinical: Student unsuited to clinical work – unable to function at expected level, shows difficulty with relationships, unreliability and/or insensitivity to patients. Unsuitability to the profession becomes apparent during clinical practice.

Wrong career choice: Student decides (with or without staff encouragement) that occupational therapy is the wrong career choice, maybe from misleading or insufficient career advice. Includes students deciding to change to another career and those who merely decide that they are not suited to occupational therapy.

Personal/domestic: Pregnancy; home circumstances changing – death, divorce, moving; family problems – parents, spouses, children, partners; cultural problems; unhappiness; homesickness of student not otherwise regarded as immature.

Immaturity: General immaturity causing problems in coping with course on the whole. Usually reflected in one or more of the other categories. Student may be unable to cope with the amount of the work on the course, gives up easily, may have loss of motivation and/or attendance. Homesickness due to immaturity and being away from home.

Other: Should be specified; includes death from whatever cause.

A similar degree of disapprobation can be levelled against other academic and vocational programmes. The following three examples from different contexts, spanning three decades and different professions, illustrate the failure to fail. Avoidance was observed in social work by Brandon and Davies in 1979. They comment 'once the decision is postponed to the second year, the pressure towards granting an automatic pass becomes almost irresistible' (p. 338). Davenhall noted in 1985 'outright failure, resulting in discontinuation of nurse training, did not appear to occur at all' (p. 106). In a study of University assessment procedures Warren-Piper (1994) notes 'the widespread reluctance to fail a candidate who has reached the end of a course' (p. 178). The longer time on a programme seems to transform what may have been a reluctance to fail into a pressure to pass.

Leniency – whether justified or unjustified – permeated Ilott's (1993) research into assessors' perspectives on the process of assigning a fail grade in occupational therapy. At training days held between 1988 and 1997 to prepare supervisors for this responsibility, over a quarter of 400+ delegates admitted to inappropriately 'allowing a student to just pass'. There was a similar proportion amongst the 30 academic and work-based volunteers who participated in a focused interview. This is an alarmingly high incidence (i.e. 25%) considering the award confers registration to practise with vulnerable people. Although much of this data is drawn from occupational therapy training, similar results can be found elsewhere, for example in the training of midwives (Fraser et al., 1997).

It is important to understand why examiners avoid their professional obligation as gatekeepers of the future practise. The five reasons why examiners give 'the benefit of the doubt' are summarised here. These are a prelude to our later discussion of the reasons why failing is so difficult (Chapters 3 and 4).

1. The conflict in values between educator and therapist. 'As therapists it is not in our nature to fail. We always look for the positive' (supervisor).
2. Lack of suitable evidence about professional unsuitability or academic weakness, which would withstand the rigours of an appeal.
3. Tension between personal suitability, i.e. the potential to be 'a good practitioner' in a practical profession with lack of academic ability to complete a degree level programme.
4. Inexperience of the examiner, which would undermine their confidence to make difficult judgements.
5. To avoid failure. 'You find reasons to push them through. For example, they've been ill or you blame yourself for not giving them enough time' (work-based supervisor).

These reasons indicate the complex set of personal, institutional and external factors which influence pass–fail decisions, and the first in the list is the reason most frequently quoted in our studies.

Prevention is better than cure

It is our view that the taboo associated with failure in professional education must be confronted to avoid incompetent, unsafe, unsuitable or
unscrupulous practitioners who are a danger to themselves and others.
The costs of moderate levels of non-completion on such courses are
relatively short lived in comparison with coping with the consequences of
professionally qualified individuals who are not adequately trained in
some basic areas. Working with incompetent colleagues has been identified as a major source of stress, creating ethical dilemmas (Barnitt, 1996).
Threshold standards are essential in professional training. It is the main
reason why the incidence of the failure to fail must be reduced. The
pattern of failures in academic and work-based education demonstrates
the learning value from a first fail. A retake assessment is an opportunity to
prove competence to deal with an increasingly challenging and changing
world. If the immediate trauma is placed in the context of the whole
training programme or a life-long career, it is reasonable to 'err on the side
of caution' and award a fail grade when threshold standards are not met.

There is much at stake. Professionals are accountable and being
brought to account. For example, newspaper headlines proclaim
'Teachers face sack if their pupils fail' (*The Times*, 1997). A minority of
incompetent professionals can do untold damage. They on their own can
ultimately destroy the reputation of a profession. Preston (1993) reporting
the results of 'The New Teacher in School: A Survey by HM Inspectors in
England and Wales 1992' stated, that around ten percent were tempera-
mentally unsuited to the profession (of teaching), frequently refusing to
acknowledge their weaknesses and resisting advice'. There is a similar
figure – between 5–10 per cent – for doctors whose performance is so
poor as to cause concern (Rosenthal, 1995). The Utting Report 'People
like us' published in 1997 found evidence that serial child abusers were
evading vetting procedures and causing misery for thousands of children
in residential and foster homes. Appropriate action, at an earlier (and
easier stage) of an undergraduate or postgraduate career could reduce
these figures. It is a critical risk management strategy within a broader
organisational context of service standards, audit and quality assurance
mechanisms.

Conclusion

Collective assessment judgements are open to public scrutiny in league
tables of results from primary schools to universities. These are quantitative measures, which are used to monitor the effectiveness, efficiency and
equity of the education system. Results are just one, but one very potent
performance indicator. They have led to a range of controversies, for
example, about the inconsistency of standards across regions for General

National Vocational Qualifications, and for A levels with schools selecting examination boards perceived to set the easiest papers. In 1994, the *Times Higher Education Supplement* reported that the Business and Technology Education Council had 'ejected 39 inspectors and struck five institutions off its list of approved training centres in a purge on low standards and cheating on courses' (Tysome, 1994). This was in response to fears about league tables and output related funding in the further education sector.

Higher education institutions have also been criticised for inconsistency with grade inflation lowering standards for first degrees in the UK (Murphy, 1995). An upper second (2:1) has become the modal degree class rather than a lower second (2:2). Between 1973–1993 the proportion of students receiving a first class degree from 'traditional, old' universities rose from 11 to 14 per cent, and those gaining an upper second rose from 31 to 44 per cent. Third class and pass degrees comprise only 5–8 per cent of awards. Interestingly, these are judged by academic staff to represent unsatisfactory performance, but not so serious as to warrant a fail (Wright, 1996). These examples illustrate public and policymakers' interest in examination results. Yet, 'in reality of course praise or blame for institutional merits or shortcomings inevitably attaches to the individuals responsible' (Clift, 1990, p. 48), i.e. the examiners. We will return to the tendency to name, blame and shame both tutors and institutions in Chapter 3 when considering the causal theory of teaching. Assessors need to be safeguarded from a position whereby failing their students can be used against them as a measure of their worth as a teacher. Tutors, whether in academic or work settings, who are required to act as assessors, need the freedom to apply appropriate threshold standards, free from other conflicting personal agendas.

The fear of appeals and complaints is another external pressure upon assessors. Students' right to 'due process' is paramount. It is as wrong to unjustly pass as it is to unjustly fail. More dissatisfied students are using local appeal or grievance procedures or the courts to seek redress for breach of contract or natural justice. The increase in number and costs is attributed to a variety of reasons. Students are members of a rights conscious, consumerist and litigious society. They, with their parents and partners, have a greater financial stake in their education which ranges from the immediate living and tuition costs, through the accumulation of debts and loans to the effect of academic results upon future earning potential. Appeals occur throughout the educational system from GCSEs to PhDs. The three most common grounds for university appeals are circumstances affecting performance which the examiners did not know about, procedural irregularities in the conduct of the examination and evidence of bias or prejudice on the part of the examiners. In most universities students may not appeal against an examiner's judgement. Nevertheless there is concern that educators will need to 'change to defensive grading and defensive lecturing' (Slapper, 1996).

Even in a consumer society where education is another commodity to be bought in the market place, students are in a relatively powerless position *vis-à-vis* assessors. They need to be treated fairly, with dignity and compassion, especially during fail scenarios. The same principles apply to assessors. We hope that this book will contribute in two ways, first through demystifying failing, and second by promoting good educational and assessment practises. Both of these are necessary to protect students and assessors from accusations of malpractice and injustice, and to further the cause of high quality university-based professional education and training.

Chapter 2
The crucial role of failure in professional training

Introduction

Assigning appropriate fail grades is especially important in professional education. Anyone involved in making such assessments is a gatekeeper of the quality of future practice, often with vulnerable service users. In this context professions embrace occupations which provide a service to others, whether teachers to children, doctors to patients, social workers to clients, or clergy to parishioners, for example. Professional education and training is more than the acquisition of special knowledge and skills. It involves socialisation with a commitment to the particular values, ethical stance and culture of the profession. Individuals become service users when they consult professionals. They do so with the expectation of competence and trust in professional conduct. This means that they have a right to expect that professionals will not abuse their relationship of power to exploit the vulnerability of the service user.

The essence of professionalism remains even in this changing era of consumerism. Charters and complaints procedures proclaim the rights and responsibilities of providers and users in public, private and voluntary sectors. The resultant rise in expectations has been mirrored by an increase in complaints and litigation. For example, the Healthcare Services Commissioners Report (1994) describes a 25 per cent increase in complaints since the previous year. Many relate to failures of communication. A study of complaints at one NHS Trust hospital noted 'Patients mostly take competence for granted and seem relatively tolerant of failures in that respect, but it is clear they resent and feel let down by rudeness and thoughtlessness' (Woodyard and Darby, 1996). There has been a parallel increase in claims for medical negligence at an estimated cost to the National Health Service (NHS) of £200 million in 1995/6 (Wilson, 1996). It could be even more expensive as more patients are injured or traumatised by their treatment than consider legal action. In the United States almost 4 per cent of admissions experience an adverse event (Vincent, 1995). Patients may claim for damages for psychiatric as well as physical injury. Interestingly, a duty of care is owed both in respect of the information given and the way it is communicated (Wilder, 1997). Other professions have also experienced a rise in complaints including education and the law. In 1994 the Solicitors Complaints Bureau estimated the cost of compensating victims of dishonest solicitors would reach nearly £30 million.

Yet instances of the abuse of professional power continue to be reported, especially involving dependent people. For example, the United Kingdom Central Council for Nursing, Midwifery and Health Visiting (UKCC, 1994) identified private nursing and residential homes for elderly people as the largest single source of complaint. Their concern highlights new problems with a mixed economy in health and social care which has replaced public sector provision with the notion of public service. The UKCC report revealed inappropriate conduct, major deficits in the organisation and supervision of clinical practice with inadequate mechanisms for maintaining standards and quality. These problems highlight why standards, especially related to professional, ethical behaviour, are vital.

While it would be unrealistic to offer a universal guarantee of safe, competent and honourable practice by all professionals all the time, the public has a right to expect rigorous enforcement of procedures toward this aspiration. This may be considered as a specific obligation upon assessors. It is a collective responsibility which is usually enshrined in codes of conduct issued by professional and statutory bodies. Guidance issued by the General Medical Council states 'You (the doctor) must protect patients when you believe that a colleague's conduct, performance or health is a threat to them' (1995, p. 6). An underlying reason why failing is so difficult can be the conflict between professional values and educator-practitioner roles. Assessors are required to negotiate this complex situation. It is our hope that an improved understanding of the conflicts and contradictions may assist assessors to take appropriate action. The next chapter examines the constellation of reasons why failing can be so stressful while this one reinforces the professional obligation to act as a gatekeeper of future standards of practice.

This chapter introduces the background to professionalism and professional education. It encompasses undergraduate and postgraduate levels where a pass grade gives eligibility to practise (or continuation through re-certification or re-registration). Clear threshold standards are particularly important where there is co-terminosity of academic award and registration as competent with a statutory or professional body to work with the public. However, competence is another problematic concept because it is such a multidimensional and elusive concept. Competence can be difficult both to define and assess in a meaningful, valid way, especially at higher, professional levels. These problems appear along the whole continuum of professional education from entry level through to advanced practice. Examiners are required to consider the needs of different stakeholders including the public, employers and higher education. The divergent needs of these different constituencies are often expressed in the terminology of production and quality. For example, the outcome of professional training should be a product or practitioner who is fit for practice, fit for purpose and fit for award to fulfil the requirements of the profession, the employer and higher education institution.

However, taking the approach of attempting to define unacceptable practice has proved a fruitful approach which has elicited more of a consensus about the components of incompetence. This approach is based upon the assumption that there is a connection between the criteria for assigning a fail grade, definitions of incompetence and competence. Inappropriate, unacceptable and unsatisfactory behaviour and attitudes seem to be easier to define than the positive competencies that constitute threshold standards. In Ilott's (1993) study respondents gave priority to global or generic personal qualities, especially professional, ethical attributes. These qualities are shared by different professions and may be considered to be at the heart of professionalism.

Professions and professional self-regulation

The privilege of self-regulation is usually accepted as one of the main characteristics of a profession. This privilege is based upon trust and accountability to the society which bestows this prerogative. There is a duty to fulfil this responsibility in a way which protects the public rather than preserving a monopoly on practice. 'Accountability is based on legal requirements and moral expectations' (Stacey, 1995, p. 35). This section summarises the key principles of statutory regulation. While the term 'moral expectations' may seem anachronistic in a consumer market-dominated society it would seem to be apt for it reflects the public expectations of good, virtuous, worthy and conscientious behaviour from professionals.

What is a profession?

There are many definitions of what counts as a profession. Occupations which attain the status of a profession are usually said to possess a set of distinguishing characteristics. These include:

- A systematic, highly specialised body of knowledge, technical skill and expert judgement, altruism with an emphasis upon service, autonomy and self-regulation.
- Control of entry to the profession through recruitment, education and qualifications at entry level and, increasingly, for continuation via schemes for continued professional development.
- Duty to maintain good standards of practice and conduct. These are expressed in guidelines and codes of ethics. This duty rests with

individual practitioners and the profession through internal disciplinary procedures which lead to 'striking off' or exclusion.

- An occupational culture with a sense of 'belonging' to a distinct, special group. The values and norms of behaviour are inculcated through the process of professional socialisation – an implicit component of the curriculum.
- The status of the profession is recognised by the society.

Responsibility and accountability are key components of professions and professionalism. This means professionals are legally responsible for their decisions and actions (Pyne, 1981).

State regulation: serving the public or a professional monopoly

Statutory regulation of health professions is well established in the United Kingdom. Medical practitioners have been subject to state registration since 1858 with the Medical Act. Regulation of pharmacists, dentists, midwives, nurses, opticians, professions supplementary to medicine (chiropodists, dieticians, medical laboratory scientific officers, occupational therapists, orthoptists, physiotherapists and radiographers, both diagnostic and therapeutic) have followed. The privilege of professional self-regulation was extended to osteopaths and chiropractors in the 1990s. Statutory regulation means Parliament formally recognises the status of the profession. It is considered to be sufficiently 'mature' to be given the right to maintain professional discipline, standards of conduct and entry into the profession. There is usually a long-arm relationship with the state which is exercised through an ultimate oversight role of the Secretary of State or Privy Council and the ability to appoint non-professionals to statutory councils and committees. This status (with the ability to avoid externally imposed statutory regulation) is being sought by other occupations which possess the characteristics of a profession such as teachers, social workers, psychologists and counsellors. For example, in 1998 the Central Council for Education and Training in Social Work is to be disbanded and replaced by the General Social Care Council. The new body will combine training and regulation of social workers.

The primary purpose of statutory regulation is to protect the public. This aim was stated by the Minister of Health about the Professions Supplementary to Medicine (PSM) Act in 1960. He declared the benefits of state registration as 'identification of trained and qualified persons with high ethical standards, not only for the purposes of the NHS, or even of other public services, but also in the eyes of the public generally' (Pickis, 1993, p. 1). This principle is reiterated in the 1996 review of the same PSM Act. 'The primary purpose of the new legislation should be to provide protection to the public through the regulation of health professions and this aim should be paramount' (JM Consulting, 1996, p. 72). The reasons were given by Sir Leon Brittan (vice-president of the European Commission and then competition commissioner) at a conference in November 1992. In response to a question about whether professions should be deregulated to increase competition he said 'when you are talking about professions you are talking about occupations which I believe are skilled, and where the degree of skill could not possibly be known by the consumer or customer, and the possibility of lack of skill can be lethal, and therefore I think it is quite unrealistic and undesirable to talk about deregulation' (Pickis, 1993, p. 7).

State registration is seen as a kite mark which sets the standard for the profession. Statutory bodies include the General Medical Council, the General Dental Council, the Boards of the Council for Professions Supplementary to Medicine, the United Kingdom Central Council for Nursing, Midwifery and Health Visiting. Registration with a statutory body sets standards of professional behaviour and for employment. These standards are achieved via three functions – registration, professional discipline and education.

Registration

A register of suitably qualified practitioners is maintained by the statutory body. Registration is a criterion for appointment in the National Health Service for example. New entrants to the profession have their name added to a public record of all registrants. Foreign qualified practitioners, whether from the European Union (EU) or elsewhere, may apply for registration. If their qualification is directly comparable, applicants from member states of the European Union and Economic Area are approved in accordance with directives related to mutual recognition of qualifications. If there is a significant difference in the professional training, they have a right to undergo a period of adaptation or to take an aptitude test. This is to ensure European applicants have an equivalent standard of competence. The same principle is applied to foreign qualified applicants who may be required to pass an assessment of professional and linguistic competence. For example, in 1995 the General Medical Council registered 10,235 new doctors. Nearly two-thirds were non-UK graduates. These figures illustrate the scope of this responsibility.

Discipline

The maintenance of professional standards and discipline is a key mechanism for protecting the public from incompetent, unsafe, sick or unscrupulous professionals. Complaints about infamous conduct or gross misconduct are dealt with by investigatory, disciplinary and health committees. Complaints can be made by members of the public, colleagues or employers. They are investigated. If the misconduct is due to some form of physical or mental impairment the complaint is usually diverted to a health committee. If there is sufficient evidence a disciplinary hearing will be held. If, at this formal, judicial hearing the registrant is found guilty of gross professional misconduct, the ultimate sanction 'striking off' the register may be imposed.

Relatively few complaints are dealt with by statutory bodies and even fewer result in the end of a career. For example, of the 1600 doctors reported annually to the GMC only about 250 reach the first stage, the Preliminary Proceedings Committee. The majority are dealt with via a letter of advice or warning. About 50 are referred to the Professional Conduct Committee. If the facts are proved then the committee decides whether the doctor is guilty of serious professional misconduct (Cogger, 1994). In 1995–96 the Preliminary Proceedings Committee of the UKCC considered 871 cases. The screening procedure eliminated 64 per cent (n=556) of the complaints against nurses (Carlisle, 1996). The cases eliminated were due to management problems (such as failure to provide supervision, lack of emergency back-up proced- ures, inappropriate delegation to junior staff, inadequate preparation for working in specialist areas, lack of proper accounting systems and sexual harassment policies) rather than 'unfitness to practise'.

The publication and revision of Statements of Conduct are another way in which statutory bodies fulfil their disciplinary functions. These can be expressed positively (thou shalt) or negatively (thou shalt not). The General Medical Council has recently adopted a positive expression. *Good Medical Practice* (1995) is a comprehensive guide to the standards expected of all medical practitioners. In contrast, the Statements of Infamous Conduct approved by the boards of the Council for Professions Supplementary to Medicine are negative. These are indicative rather than detailed. They indicate the kind of behaviour which is serious enough to bring the profes- sion into disrepute, i.e. which is infamous in a professional respect. Appendix 1 contains the introduction and statements for the Occupational Therapists Board. The statements are broad for two reasons. It is impossible to compile a definitive list of proscribed actions or inactions which would be dangerous (Pyne, 1981). Who would have legislated for the nurse (Beverly Allitt) who was found guilty of murdering children in her care? Second, each complaint is judged 'on its own merits and in the light of the registrant's duty to have proper regard to the welfare of the patient so that the health or safety of the patient is not endangered' (Occupational Therapists Board, 1996). This means there are no precedents. It also recognises the impor- tance of context. This is important because 'practitioners are constantly engaged in the exercise of professional judgement and responsibility and often in an imperfect environment' (Pyne, 1981) whether due to excessive pressure of work, unclear policies or inadequate management. Table 2.1 compares the topics within the statements for seven of the nine boards of the Council for Professions Supplementary to Medicine (CPSM). The table excludes the statements for the two new boards (Board for Prosthetists and Orthotists and Board for Arts Therapists) which were established in 1997.

Table 2.1 Comparison of topics identified as infamous practice by seven boards of the Council for Professions Supplementary to Medicine

Infamous conduct	Chiropodists	Dietitians	Medical laboratory scientific officers	Occupational therapists	Orthoptists	Physiotherapists	Radiographers
Endanger health and safety of patient	✓	✓	✓	✓	✓	✓	✓
Scope of practice – only practice in those fields in which been trained	✓	✓	–	–	✓	–	–
Advertising	✓	✓	✓	✓	✓	✓	✓
Sell, accept commission for sale of goods or improper promotion of goods	✓	✓	–	–	✓	✓	–
Teach or examine students from an institution not recognised by the board	✓	–	–	–	–	–	–
Improper delegation to non-state registered practitioner	✓	–	–	–	–	–	–
Confidentiality	✓	✓	✓	✓	✓	✓	✓
Prescription for treatment from/or communication with a registered medical, dental or veterinary practitioner	–	✓	✓	–	✓	✓	✓
Cross infection – HIV, AIDS, hepatitis	–	✓	–	–	–	–	✓
Invasive procedures without training	–	✓	–	–	–	–	–
Communicate with patients	–	✓	–	–	–	–	–
Purport to diagnose or treat	–	–	✓	–	–	–	✓
Falsify or suppress or disclose results of investigations	–	–	✓	–	–	–	✓

Education

The third function relates to the approval of educational institutions, courses, examinations and qualifications. Institutions are required to be properly organised and equipped for conducting the course of professional training. The course, examination and qualification are required to ensure those who obtain it possess sufficient knowledge and skills to be safe, competent practitioners. This is how individual assessors are linked with the legislative framework. The assessment of 'competence to practise' is not merely to relieve an assessor's 'anxiety or insecurity' (Holt, 1970). It is a crucial part of the vocational certification process which is entrusted to the profession by society (Rowntree, 1987).

This leaves professional and statutory bodies (PSB) with the prime responsibility to be guardians of their own standards. When professional education is conducted in partnership with universities this leads to a complex set of challenges, including the role of the external examiner. Warren-Piper (1994), in a recent book devoted almost entirely to an evaluation of the external examiner system, comments cogently: 'The professional bodies, in these instances, are exercising their right to restrict entry to a monopolistic body and their duty to ensure that members are carefully selected and properly trained. When they appoint an external examiner to an examination conducted by a university, they are not policing the professional conduct of the other examiners, they are only ensuring a proper standard of admission to the professional body' (p. 5). The management of multiple roles by external examiners is recognised by the new Quality Assurance Agency for Higher Education (QAA). They note that 'accreditation is about satisfying the PSB that a programme ensures that a successful student has crossed the threshold of immediate occupational competence' (QAA, 1998, p. 18). The importance of external examiners is a further aspect of the assessment process to which we will return in Chapter 6.

Other countries and professions do this too, but ...

Other countries have regulatory systems which may be placed in three broad categories. These are:

- Registration whereby those who are declared eligible by a public body have their names entered upon a register kept for that purpose as occurs in the UK.
- Code-based system where education, training and discipline are directly controlled by a government department, either nationally or regionally.
- Licensing system which involve boards with state level accountability issuing a 'licence to practise' to those who are eligible.

There are practical and philosophical differences between these three legislative approaches to professional regulation (Berrie, 1998). The key features of registration as they apply in the UK have been described earlier in this chapter. While the professions have a degree of autonomy it can never be absolute because of the requirement that all organised groups be held accountable to the public interest (ultimately via the Secretary of State or Privy Council). Although the registration system is liberal and flexible, it also leaves a certain amount to chance and to the good will of the professionals themselves. A code-based system operates in some European countries. This is where education, training and discipline are controlled directly by a government department, either nationally as in France and the Netherlands, or regionally as in Germany. The code-based system is based on the philosophy that all individual citizens and organised groups have rights and duties, and are subject to the 'general will'. Only practitioners qualifying from approved schools have a right to practise the profession. They are bound by the legal code (which is an integral part of the whole legal code) which also prescribes the scope of practice. This system protects the public by preventing all those who are not properly qualified from practising. It can be rigid for changing the scope of practice – what practitioners can do – means changing the law of the land. The third system involves licensing boards issuing a 'licence to practise'. In the USA and other federal systems, boards are at state level and are accountable either directly to the governor or to the state legislature. As with the registration system, the licence (which is issued to, and can be displayed by each practitioner), can be withdrawn in the same way as a registrant can be 'struck off' the register held by the official body. There is an important difference. Registration does not close the profession to all but those who are qualified and registered, whereas licensing effectively closes it by giving only those who are eligible (and have paid their fee) a licence to practise the profession.

The principles of registration, licensure or code-based systems seem laudable. Protecting the public is a concern which is shared across the globe. Yet it has been challenged. Low suggests it perpetuates a professional monopoly, reflecting a paternalistic attitude which underpins a medical model of illness. 'To the extent one protects a person from harm produced by causes beyond the persons' knowledge and control, the intervention has plausible claim to being morally justified, for the choices are substantially non-voluntary' (Low, 1992, p. 374). Knowledge-based occupations of 'experts' are able to retain control even when their autonomy is challenged by managerial authority (Freidson, 1994). Professions, by establishing a monopoly of (and access to) specific knowledge, are seen as just another interest group in search of economic reward and status. Stacey's research in medicine 'suggests professional self-regulation will always be likely to favour the profession over the public' (1995, p. 45). She recommends a 'new kind of professionalism, in which service is the first priority and in which other health care workers and patients were recognised as members of the health team having equal worth' (p. 47).

Although we support this inclusive rather than monopolistic approach, we believe there must be rigorous enforcement (at all stages from pre-registration to continuous competence). The failure to protect vulnerable clients from the range of abuses perpetrated by a few unscrupulous professionals is to be condemned. No qualification or examination can be a guarantee against such abuses of power. This is why we believe all have a responsibility to confront the failure of students or staff to attain or maintain the standard of competence the public has a right to expect. This obligation demands surveillance and action not the 'defensiveness (and) ... strong sense of professional solidarity' (Stacey, 1995) which prevents 'whistleblowing' or 'shopping colleagues'. The incidence is low – Rosenthal estimates 5 per cent of doctors are clinically incompetent (1995) – but the costs are high. Failing students who do not achieve threshold standards could be viewed as a preventative strategy. This could change the situation, bluntly summarised by a retired professor of surgery: 'Our training doesn't include getting the "buggers" out of our system. We don't emphasise professionalism right from the start' (quoted in Rosenthal, 1995).

Threshold standards and beyond: a continuum of incompetence – competence

Judgements require a clear definition of threshold standards or competence. These are elusive, problematic concepts. Threshold standards were considered by the Higher Education Quality Council (HEQC, 1995) as part of their work on comparability of academic standards and definitions of 'graduateness'. If the recommendation of the Dearing report (1997) are followed through they will continue to be a concern of the new Quality Assurance Agency (QAA). The National Committee of Inquiry into Higher Education charged the QAA 'to work with institutions to establish small, expert teams to provide benchmark information on standards, in particular threshold standards, operating within the framework of qualifications, and completing the task by 2000' (1997, p. VII paragraph 49). The HEQC found that 'the concept of threshold standards is unclear ... except in professional subjects where the award of a degree carries a licence to practise' (1995, p. 4).

Where there is co-terminosity of award with licence to practise students are expected to meet the triple criteria of fitness for practise, purpose and award (HEQC/NHSE, 1996). This is to fulfil the standards set by the profession, employers and higher education. These are defined as:

• Fitness for practice: determines registration or re-registration as a professional. Judgements derive from professional opinion about the scope and nature of practice which tend to change in an evolutionary or incremental way in response to advances in knowledge, technology, service organisation and policy initiatives. The conferring of licence to practise represents a long-term endorsement of an individual's capabilities and capacities which may not correspond with an employers' requirements. Fitness for practice is the major concern of the professional and statutory bodies.

- Fitness for purpose: fulfils the employers' requirements. It represents the competencies and capabilities which the employee demonstrates in the workplace. This criteria underpins the specification of occupational standards and National Vocational Qualifications. Fitness for purpose is context-specific in that it describes the knowledge, skills, attitudes and attributes necessary for a particular job at a particular time. However, core or key skills such as adaptability and flexibility are increasingly prized so the organisation can respond to the pace of change.
- Fitness for award: relates to academic judgements about attainment in learning which are certified via qualifications. In the further education sector in United Kingdom there are now more than 17,000 different qualifications awarded by more than 500 awarding bodies. Unsurprisingly, this plethora of academic and vocational qualifications is poorly understood by students, parents and employers. The problems with articulating the learning outcomes for degree classifications and the comparability of standards between different higher education establishments was a primary reason for the current interest in graduateness.

These three complementary demands of fitness for practise, purpose and award are important. Yet in the context of professional training 'competence to practise' is likely to take precedence. This is because the boundary between competence and incompetence is more critical than ranking for the determination of academic honours (Newble, Jolly and Wakeford, 1994). Work-based staff are in an ideal position to appraise the integration of knowledge, skill and ethical, professional conduct in real, naturalistic settings. Yet, these are often the least prepared and valued members of the training community because their primary responsibility is working with service users.

Horror stories as a reminder of the need for minimum standards of competence

Accusations and evidence of malpractice, negligence or misconduct are costly for all parties. The cost may be measured in lives, distress or monetary terms. The following extreme examples from different professions received much media attention during the 1990s. The case of the nurse Beverly Allitt, convicted of murdering four children and harming nine others, is one of the most tragic. The front page of *The Times* reported how she 'worked at

Grantham and District Hospital as a state enrolled nurse for 59 days in 1991 during which she killed three babies – the youngest eight weeks old – and a boy aged 11. She also tried to kill another three children, assaulted a further six, some of whom have been left severely brain damaged' (18 May 1993, p.1). Allitt was diagnosed as having Munchausen's Syndrome which developed into Munchausen's By Proxy. Her history of self-inflicted injuries – to injuring others- for attention included taking 94 days off sick during 1990 which delayed her qualification as a nurse.

An editorial in *The Times* on the next day (19 May 1993, p. 17) noted the similarity of career patterns between Allitt and a residential social worker, Frank Beck. At the 'end of Britain's biggest child abuse case' in November 1991 he was given five life sentences (Ford, 1994). Beck was described as conducting reign of terror physically, psychologically and sexually abusing 200 children over a 13-year period while head of three children's homes in Leicester. The editorial condemned the 'unacceptably slack recruitment procedures...and supervision' concluding that 'the safety of the public must take precedence over "fair" employment practises in the public sector'.

There are more examples taken from a broadsheet newspaper which we assume to be less sensational than the tabloid press. Two headlines from *The Times* about dentists encapsulate the profit – 'dentist who made £1 million is struck off' (21 January 1997, p. 3) – and pain – 'dentist's patients win £2 million damages' (10 September 1997, p.5). Both related to dentists who carried out unnecessary work for profit which left patients physically and mentally damaged. The abuse of trust by clergy from the Roman Catholic Church, the Anglican Church and the Methodist Church were all reported in 1997. It ranged from child sex abuse to sexual abuse and harassment of adults by clergy and lay workers. Sexual harassment came to media attention in the legal profession too. On the same page 3 February 1995 *The Times*, p. 3 reported the case of a barrister who had been suspended for three months for harassing a client and a solicitor's clerk, and a head of police training college who had been demoted for 'allegedly telling women trainees that he would help their careers in exchange for sexual favours'.

In addition to examples of unprofessional conduct and unethical behaviour (especially doing more harm than good) there are those which relate to competence. In May 1997 the new Secretary of State for Education and Employment, Mr David Blunkett issued a warning to failing schools, incompetent teachers and head teachers. He stated 'we absolutely will not tolerate underperformance...where progress is inadequate the idea of a "fresh start" – closing and reopening [the school] with a new leadership and a new mission – is considered' (*The Times*, 20 May 1997, p. 22). There was a judgement against an educational psychologist for failing 'to diagnose dyslexia [which] amounted to a failure to exercise the degree and skill expected of an ordinarily competent member of the profession' with the local authority vicariously liable for that negligence (*The Times* Law Report, 10 October 1997, p. 39).

The Medical (Professional Performance) Act 1995 which came into effect on 1 September 1997 extended the jurisdiction of the General Medical Council to investigate cases where there is evidence that a doctor's general performance is seriously deficient.

Previously, the GMC's powers only covered those cases where a doctor's fitness to practise was seriously impaired by ill health, or where allegations of serious misconduct were made, or where a doctor was convicted of a criminal offence. In 1990–91 the estimated cost of medical negligence claims for England was £52.3 million (Fenn, Hermans and Dingwall, 1994). This had risen to £200 million for the NHS in 1995–96 (Wilson, 1996). These fiscal costs pale into insignificance when compared with extreme abuses of power and position. Such calculations do not quantify the emotional costs associated with misdiagnosis, or mal- or no treatment. These are expressed in emotive headlines such as 'short cut to jail for surgeons' (*The Times*, 28 June 1994, p. 37) due to the increase in prosecutions for medical manslaughter; or 'smear blunder hospital accused over three deaths' (*The Times*, May 21 1997, p. 8) and 'surgeon who removed the wrong organs is struck off' (*The Times*, 10 October 1996, p. 3). The latter refers to removal from the medical register of the General Medical Council.

Approximately 1,600 of a community of 130,000 medical practitioners in Britain (Smith, 1997) are reported to the GMC annually with reference to their professional conduct. Donaldson describes his experience of dealing with problem doctors as 'difficult, distasteful, time consuming and acrimonious work. For these reasons the temptation to avert one's gaze ... is at times very great ... I have no doubt that many employers do look away when they should not' (1994, p. 281). This statement highlights a tendency to avoid, rather than confront, incompetent, unsafe or unscrupulous practitioners. In an editorial in the *British Medical Journal*, Smith comments

'no country has an adequate system for managing problem doctors. British doctors, for instance, have been regulated by the General Medical Council for well over a century, but the Council is only now introducing a system for dealing with poorly performing doctors. In the United States problem doctors can skip from state to state, always one jump ahead of the statutory machinery. Swedish researchers conclude that there has not been enough emphasis in the Nordic countries on tracking problem doctors and taking preventative action. The Canadians observe that bad doctors are insensitive to the threat of discipline whereas good doctors are needlessly worried about it' (1997, p. 481).

This chapter highlights the importance of taking preventative action across all the professions.

Competency conundrum, or how do you define competence?

These examples highlight the importance of assuring both entry level and continued competence. Although the 'competency movement' has dominated the last decade it remains a problematic term which creates controversy rather than consensus. The debate is contained in other texts such as Eraut (1994) and Barnett (1994). A pragmatic approach is adopted here. Although different conceptualisations with pros and cons will be summarised the key is whether they help assessors make difficult judgements. This means the definition must 'capture the holistic richness of professional practice' (Hager and Gonczi, 1996, p. 15). The different approaches to competence add to the conundrum. These include task-based or behaviourist, general, transferable attributes and the integrated approach which seeks to combine the best of both. The main features of these three approaches are summarised below.

Behaviourist approach

In task-based or behaviourist approaches competence specifies what needs to be done to achieve the job purpose The tasks which underpin performance are detailed as discrete entities. The result can represent a simple, clear and comprehensive description of the behaviours associated with each task or outcome. This approach has been much criticised for reducing professional knowledge to a long list of atomised, technical tasks. It ignores underlying attributes, group processes, context specificity of performance in the real world and the complexity of professional judgements. This conceptualisation, which derives from functional job analysis (Fine, 1988), underpins the model adopted by the former National Council for Vocational Qualifications (now Qualifications and Curriculum Authority). Work-based qualifications intended to have 'parity of esteem' with academic awards have developed during the last decade to provide a coherent qualification structure, improve the capability of the workforce and thus the competitiveness of UK plc. The initial emphasis was upon craft and technician qualifications. There is increasing recognition that an outcome-based model of competence is inappropriate for higher level occupations. This model does not accommodate the distinctive features of professional practice where individuals combine autonomy (valued as clinical or academic freedom, for example) with accountability. Professional practice requires a substantial body of knowledge and understanding necessary for occupational competence, problem solving, handling uncertainty, the unexpected and ethical decision making (DfEE, 1996).

Attributional approach

A second model concentrates on the general, underlying attributes of the person which are considered to be necessary for effective performance.

Such personal qualities include critical thinking, problem solving, proactivity and self-confidence. It is assumed these general attributes can be transferred from situation to situation or provide the platform for the development of specific, job-related attributes. This model underpins research to identify the attributes of effective managers, graduates and employees for example. While there may be differences in emphasis due to variations in the workplace – both actual and organisational culture – lists of generic competencies are remarkably similar across countries, time and occupations. They may be split into personal attributes and interactive attributes (Harvey et al., 1997). Personal attributes comprise:

- intellect
- knowledge
- willingness and ability to learn
- flexibility and adaptability to respond to change
- self-regulatory skills such as self-discipline, time keeping and planning, self-motivation and self-assurance.

Interactive attributes include interpersonal skills, teamworking and communication skills.

There are two main criticisms of the general attribute model of competence. First, the generic competencies may not exist because of the context and subject specificity of expertise. Individuals demonstrate little capacity to transfer expertise from one area of activity to another (Gonczi, 1994). Expertise is sensitive to, and specific to the context. The second problem is practical rather than conceptual. Are generic competencies learnt, inherited or both?

Integrated approach

Finally, the integrated approach to competence attempts to combine the best of the other two models. Gonczi (1994) defines integrated competency as the complex combination of knowledge, attitudes, values and skills necessary for safe, intelligent performance in specific situations. It acknowledges the importance of the context, professional judgement, clinical reasoning, ethics and that there may be more than one way of practising competently. This definition mirrors that of capability, which is 'an integration of knowledge, skills and personal qualities used effectively and appropriately in response to varied, familiar and unfamiliar circumstances' (Stephenson, 1994, p. 3).

An integrated approach to competence underpinned the development of competency-based standards for a range of professions in Australia. The aims were similar to those for National Vocational Qualifications in the United Kingdom in that standards provide an open and equitable assessment of those educated overseas and with work experience against agreed, public standards of performance. There is articulated training and progression within industries (Heywood, Gonczi and Hager, 1992). The main difference is the starting point. In Australia the standards were developed by the professions. In the United Kingdom an occupational map, which defined the overall purpose, scope and boundaries of some employment sectors, was the starting point. This illustrates the focus upon outcome or function rather than the professions traditionally responsible for doing what needs to be done.

Competence to practise

Integrated competence is holistic. It captures the richness of professional practise through inference from the performance of complex, demanding key tasks. Holism is also a feature of definitions of 'competence to practise'. This is defined by the CPSM (1979) as 'the possession of knowledge, skills and attitudes enabling an individual to perform fully in a basic professional role. It includes performance of tasks and relationships which meet specific objectives of safety, efficiency and social acceptance in the environments normally encountered'. It comprises knowledge (intellectual competence, problem solving ability, appropriate application of), skills (psychomotor, the actual quality of performance) and attitudes (interpersonal skills and concerns for the clients welfare). Another important component is safety or safe practise which Caney defines as the ability to recognise, select and act appropriately upon significant cues because 'failure to notice or appreciate the significance of relevant cues may lead to ineffective, inappropriate, inaccurate or dangerous treatment which are the marks of incompetence' (1983, p. 302).

A definition of 'competence to practise' is one which is decided by and can be recognised, nationally and internationally, by members of any profession (Worth-Butler, Fraser and Murphy, 1995). It is a relative term only having meaning in the context of use, for example as an entry level practitioner. Although rather vague when compared with occupational standards or competency-based standards, this conceptualism suggests there may be an 'unspoken consensus on what constitutes competence' (Davies and van der Gaag, 1992, p. 210). This agreement, both within and between professions was apparent when incompetence, rather than competence, was the figure of attention.

Incompetence: an important construct

There is a plethora of literature presenting the philosophical or practical pros and cons about the different conceptualisations of competence, yet there is little about incompetence. This seems to be changing. There is increasing concern about incompetence, errors and mistakes. This is for many reasons, including the growth of consumerism, the need for cost containment and the expanding web of formal regulation. These increase accountability and challenge autonomy. Some are supported by the professions involved while others are more contentious. For example, the

Medical (Professional Performance) Act 1995 was based upon proposals made by the General Medical Council. This is an example of the statutory body 'kite marking' practice and dealing with poor standards as part of their 'duty to protect the public against the genially incompetent as well as the deliberate wrongdoers' (Law Report, 1995). In the area of initial teacher training the Teacher Training Agency (TTA) has closed university-based teacher training courses on the basis of evidence from the Office for Standards in Education (OFSTED) inspections. This provides an even more extreme example of guarding professional standards, allowing one-off judgements by a visiting team of government inspectors, not simply to challenge the judgements of professional tutors, but to take the most extreme action by closing down entire courses and, in the case of Le Saint Union College in Southampton, a whole institution with a long history of involvement in the initial training of school teachers.

The primary duty of safeguarding professional entry standards, however, starts with the gatekeeping role of assessors. Subsequently, this section focuses upon the criteria for assigning a fail grade in academic and work settings and the added difficulty of differentiating between a pass and fail grade with borderline students. Also, how these criteria correlate with definitions of competence and incompetence.

Criteria for a fail grade

Identifying criteria for assigning a fail grade as a baseline definition of incompetence

Identifying the constituents of incompetence was one part of Ilott's (1993) study into the assessors' perspective on awarding a fail grade. It drew upon the assumption that competence 'is recognisable more by its absence than by readily measurable behaviours' (Burrows, 1989, p. 222). The intention was to describe the knowledge, skills and attitudes considered to be unsatisfactory or inappropriate so as to complement existing assessments of 'competence to practise'. Positive evidence of competence and incompetence are necessary for good judgements. As the research progressed, a general consensus became apparent both within occupational therapy and other health care professions about the criteria for a fail grade. The constituents of incompetence seem to apply across disciplines, at entry level and for continued practice.

Criteria for failure, incompetence and competence

The reasons for assigning a fail grade are similar to definitions of incompetence, which in turn is the obverse of competence to practise. This neatness is not contrived but a logical outcome of scrutinising the same problem from different perspectives. In this section each concept will be defined and compared with the multiprofessional literature.

Dictionary definitions of fail, failed, failing and failure share the words 'unsuccessful', 'tried but failed', 'not good enough', 'non-performance' and to 'not pass'. These terms are expanded into an array of implicit and explicit assessment constructs used to define failure. Table 2.2 contains those obtained during the syndicate groups with 475 work-based and

Table 2.2 Differentiating between a pass and fail grade: results from syndicate groups with 475 work-based and academic assessors at 23 failure workshops held in the United Kingdom and Sweden between 1989–1997

Construct	Elements: components of construct in order of frequency	Frequency of report	Percentage %
Unprofessional behaviour	Lack of initiative, irresponsible, unprofessional, unreliable, misconduct, breaches of confidentiality, inappropriate appearance, untrustworthy	170	22
Skills deficit	Interpersonal, communication, general, practical, clinical skills	122	15.5
Personality	Over and under confidence, lack of insight, immaturity, judgmental	77	10
Knowledge	Failure to apply, inadequate knowledge, understanding and responsibility	72	9
Unsafe	General – related to patients, self and others, health and safety, dangerous practices	60	8
Attitudes	Inappropriate to patients, staff, profession and team	57	7
Motivation	Disinterest, lack of effort and commitment	48	6
Feedback	Inability or unwillingness to change in response to feedback	46	6
Self-management	Poor self-evaluation, time and task management	35	4
Miscellaneous	Comments from team, stage of training, intuition, combination of factors	33	4
Unmet objectives	Failure to achieve learning outcomes set by course, setting or self	30	4
Personal and cultural factors	Mental health, discriminatory attitudes	23	3
Global criteria	Employability	12	1.5

academic assessors. Each construct is multifaceted. The first and most important was professional unsuitability.

Professional unsuitability

This is another broad concept which is easier to approve than define. Unprofessional behaviour was the most frequently reported reason for assigning a fail grade by the syndicate groups. It comprises lack of initiative, irresponsibility, unprofessionalism, unreliability and misconduct as a general term. Some behaviour was specified. This included unpunctuality, dishonesty, aggression, theft, fraud, abuse including alcohol and cruelty, breaches of confidentiality, inappropriate appearance, untrustworthy, unethical behaviour and passive or manipulative avoidance of situations.

Professional unsuitability also figures in the literature. Some personal and professional qualities are embodied in Codes of Ethics, Professional Conduct and Statements of Professional Misconduct, or Infamous Conduct. The components mirror the two most frequent problems among senior hospital doctors (Donaldson, 1994). These were poor attitude and disruptive or irresponsible behaviour and lack of commitment to duties. Brandon and Davies (1979) defined unprofessional attitudes as lying, breaching confidentiality, causing unjustifiable offence to clients, unpunctuality, inadequate standards of attendance and record keeping. Such 'abstract moral traits' including loyalty, honesty and reliability are consistently highly rated by employers (Hyland, 1991). These qualities are also valued by lecturers, especially when confronted with academic offences such as cheating, copying, collusion, breaches of confidentiality and plagiarism. Bradshaw and Lowenstein (1990) comment 'the destructive behaviour pattern evident in students who routinely demonstrate unethical actions is likely to carry over from the classroom to the clinical setting. Student honesty and integrity are essential to safe, competent professional practice' (p. 12).

Poor communication skills

Deficits in communication, interpersonal and to a lesser extent, practical skills was the second most frequently mentioned reason for assigning a fail grade. It occurs and recurs in the interprofessional, international literature. Deficiencies in communication and interpersonal skills were the largest categories in Holmes, Mann and Hennan's (1990) definition of fitness and aptitude for medicine. This is unsurprising. 'Bedside manner' or the equivalent 'therapeutic use of self' is the primary tool of many health and social care professions. Failure of communication and staff attitude form a significant proportion of complaints made by patients using hospital and primary care services (Allsop and Mulcahy, 1996). Interestingly communication is one of three key skill areas now being emphasised in a wide variety of frameworks for education and training nationally. The other two are information technology and application of number. Evidence from Murphy et al. (1997) suggests that students following a wide range of university-based courses cannot be assumed to have even fairly modest competence in communication skills.

Dangers: unsafe and lack of learning

The danger of over-confidence leading to practising beyond the limits of knowledge links the criteria of safety, knowledge and personal factors. Safety was mentioned infrequently by occupational therapists. It seemed to be an implicit criteria whereas it was explicit in the medical, nursing, physiotherapy and radiography professions. For example, Table 2.3 contains the information from the first page of the clinical assessment for radiography students at the University of Derby (1994).

Safety is multifaceted. Trust is an important component. A supervisor defined this as 'can you leave the student with the patients for 30 seconds?'. Safety involves more than respecting health and safety policies. It requires the ability to recognise significant cues and act appropriately, and also, an awareness of limitations to prevent practising beyond the level of knowledge or skills. This is one of the criteria for unsafe practise adopted by Darragh et al. (1986). Hausman et al. (1990) revealed a significant relationship between over-confidence and lower examination scores in paediatric residents.

Although lack of profession-specific knowledge figures on the checklist of 'how to spot a bad teacher' (Scott-Clarke and Hymas, 1996) it was not a prominent reason for failing. Priority was given to the process of, and attitude toward learning. This underpins life-long learning and therefore continued professional development. Life-long learning is another area currently being stressed within a wide range of key skills developments, often under a heading such as 'managing own learning' (Murphy et al., 1997). Learning encompasses evidence of improvement in a profile of results, the ability to apply and integrate knowledge in practice settings, the ability (and motivation) to learn from mistakes and change. This is

Table 2.3 Clinical assessment for radiography students at the University of Derby (1994) related to automatic fails

---

Instructions: Assessors must record an automatic fail and terminate the assessment immediately if the student:

---

a) fails to correctly identify the patient
b) fails to recognise the possibility of pregnancy
c) attempts to use a technique which may aggravate the patient's condition
d) prepares to examine the incorrect region of the patient
e) fails to adequately protect the patient from radiation
f) commits a serious breach of professional ethics
g) commits a serious breach of professional conduct

another common and consistent criteria being noted over time by Towle (1954), Wong (1979) and Ford and Jones (1987) for example.

Implicit criteria

Implicit assessment constructs do not appear in course documentation. They are subtle, subjective factors which, although personal, seem to be shared by many assessors. These include the temptation to reward effort, interest and hard work even though threshold standards have not been achieved. There is also a global definition of competence encapsulated by two questions 'would I employ him/her?' and 'would I want him/her to treat me or my family?' These simple questions epitomise fitness for purpose and practice from the employers' and consumers' perspectives respectively. While these questions appear in the literature (Green, 1991) and have been used to validate assessment tools (Crocker et al., 1975) they are usually implicit rather than explicit assessment criteria. A variable mix of implicit and explicit criteria was noted by Eraut and Cole (1993) who observed 'there was a clear implication in many professions that standards were basically of a tacit nature, but nevertheless understood by seasoned professionals' (p. 23).

Miscellaneous criteria: do different criteria apply in different settings?

There are many obvious and subtle differences between academic and work settings. Making the most of each, especially the inter-relationship between theory and practice, is one of the greatest challenges for professional education. In 1979 Howard described the additional, special problems of vocational training in social work. They are still relevant and applicable to other professions. The problems included an assessment criteria which is strictly educational in one instance and very much related to practise in another, with the different criteria being appropriate at different times and also being a cause of dispute between those making the judgements. The difficulty is aggravated because the basis for such judgement is rarely stated explicitly. Benchmarks are therefore the first of three miscellaneous criteria.

Benchmarks

The first difference relates to the benchmarks against which performance is supposed to be judged. 'Supposed' is added as a rider because failure to achieve the learning outcomes expressed in course documentation (workplace report form or answer and marking guidelines, for example) was mentioned infrequently as a reason for failure (Table 2.2). In work settings the objectives may be set by the educational establishment according to the stage of training, developed by the department to be specific to the site or negotiated with the student to match their experience, ability and aspirations or a combination of all three. The learning objectives and work placement report form may be used as a basis for formative and summative assessment. They can communicate assessors' expectations and act as a 'baseline for supervisors and students' (supervisor). The achievement, non-achievement and plateaux in learning can then be monitored during regular weekly supervision sessions with specific feedback and action planning. 'They concentrate our thoughts. Is the student doing this? If not, they do not progress until the objective has been achieved' (supervisor).

Marking and answer guidelines provide an equivalent structure for academic staff. This makes assessment 'easier because it is based on knowledge or skills. We have marking guidelines' (lecturer). Specific criteria, independent double-marking by internal assessors and verification by external examiners can all be used to support the credibility of academic assessments (Murphy, 1989). However, this can lead to a 'spurious objectivity' (Stone, 1982, p. 103). It does not prevent assessors exercising judgement which goes beyond subject-specific knowledge and focuses upon the student's potential to 'be a good practitioner'. This global factor may determine the outcome because marking guidelines are 'flexible, for external consumption. I use my gut reaction, based on experience and personal standards. If the failure would result in termination of training, I will ask myself whether the student will make a good occupational therapist. If the answer is no, then I do not try to find extra marks' (lecturer). Potential is another implicit assessment criteria. It mirrors fitness for practice and purpose but seems to override fitness for award.

Professionalism

The comparatively easy assessment of certain scientific or mathematical academic subjects may be contrasted with the assessment of professionalism and the professional skills in work settings. These depend upon subjective judgements and are much more difficult to define. There may also be less excuses for failure. Failure cannot in these circumstances be blamed upon lack of revision or poor examination technique. It may be perceived as 'total, they feel a failure. As who they are – as a therapist. This seems more profound and disturbing' (work-place organiser). Professionalism needs also to be demonstrated in the academic setting. It could be argued this academic context, where the predominant role set is student with the associated norms and expectations, is inappropriate for judging professional suitability. Yet the potential to be a 'good practitioner' is a key criterion for borderline students. This dilemma may be considered from the perspective of learning as a rite of passage (White, 1989) in which the student is expected to quickly become 'enculturated' (Eisenhart, Behm and Romagnano 1990), to demonstrate through appearance and behaviour the accepted, conventional requirements of the profession.

The elusive, yet critical nature of professional suitability means a structured, monitoring scheme is needed. Professional unsuitability should be recognised as a valid reason for failing a student on a vocational course in a higher education institution, and ultimately the course itself must be judged for its own suitability. Professionalism is paramount for public protection and as such it should take precedence over academic attainment. However, students retain their right to natural justice. This means procedures must be clear, open and accountable. For example, health and attendance requirements need to be stated (and verified) at selection and at the beginning of each academic year. This follows one of the recommendations of the Clothier Report (Clothier, Macdonald and Shaw, 1994) otherwise known as the Allitt Inquiry. This stated that applicants for nursing 'who show one or more of these patterns (excessive absence through sickness, excessive use of counselling or medical facilities, or self-harming behaviour such as attempted suicide, self-laceration or eating disorders) should not be accepted for training until they have shown the ability to live an independent life without professional support and have been in stable employment for at least two years' (para. 5.5.16). Monitoring also applies to legislation such as the Rehabilitation of Offenders Act (1974) especially if the profession is 'excepted' for spent convictions and police checks for staff and students who work with children. Any concerns or untoward incidents should be documented on the student's file. A detailed record, dated and signed by all parties provides both contemporaneous and cumulative evidence. This may be required at a formal disciplinary hearing or appeal. It also demonstrates 'due process' – the student has been treated fairly. Assessment criteria should include specific statements and standards related to professional, ethical behaviour. These may be based upon the professions' code of conduct or contain examples of professional unsuitability and professional misconduct. Whatever the system, there should be procedural consistency and constancy of performance criteria to respect the rights of all parties.

Evidence

Academic assessments are often based primarily upon written evidence rather than the incidental, ephermal evidence gained during observation and questioning in work settings. Assignments in some cases may be read anonymously (using number rather than named scripts), re-read and moderated by internal and external examiners. The support gained from such shared decision making is just one of the organisational structures which substantiate academic criteria. Others include the reassurance gained from independent checks carried out by external examiners and formal ratification procedures employed by the examination boards.

Differentiation at the margins between pass and fail

Perhaps the most difficult assessment judgements in professional education courses occurs at the margins between a pass and a fail grade. A clear
fail may be obvious but the borderline between a pass and fail is almost
certainly going to be problematic. It is known that there is a tendency to
give the student 'the benefit of the doubt', to avoid a fail grade because of
the uncertainty or lack of conclusive, substantive evidence (Ilott, 1993;
Fraser et al.,1997). The criteria used by staff at this juncture include global
and specific factors. The decision is usually subject to scrutiny by internal
and external examiners. It is susceptible to external pressures which can
result in a change, usually in the direction of leniency so a pass is awarded.
Chapter 4 discusses the reasons why fail grades can be difficult.

In this section the focus is upon the assessors' criteria when judging
'marginal students' and how they differentiate between pass and fail
grades. Occupational therapy assessors identified three criteria – potential, safety and effort – as critical when making judgements about borderline students. Although similar to those for awarding a fail grade these are
more salient.

Potential

The first relates to potential, either to learn or to be a 'good practitioner'.
Potential to learn incorporated several factors including:

- effort and consistency
- performance impaired by extenuating personal circumstances
- any evidence of improvement based upon current abilities and track
  record
- whether the student was able and willing to learn from their mistakes.

This example, given by a work-based supervisor, links the two aspects
of potential. 'A borderline means the student has shown potential to
improve. We think they will become competent in time. They are able to
retain and use what they learn but they take longer to learn. With a failing
student you have to constantly repeat instructions, write step-by-step
guidelines and use a variety of teaching methods. But they still do not
"pick it up". Also, whether there is a match between what the student has
actually done and the case-notes.' The last sentence hints at unreliability
and untrustworthiness – qualities implicit in professionalism – or being a
'good practitioner'.

Safety

This was described as the 'ultimate' criterion by a work-based assessor. It is
based upon the subjective element of trust, whether the assessor can trust

the student to work with service users. An important component is insight into the limits of their own knowledge and skill. Especially, whether the students are aware of the dangers of practising beyond the boundaries of their competence and whether they are willing to seek advice. A manager summarised the risks associated with over-confidence: 'A student may be good on paper but not really understand. Such a façade is dangerous because they will be judged as competent on their presentational skills. Also, they do not know what they do not know and this is dangerous.'

Effort

Effort was the third criteria commonly used to differentiate between a pass and fail grade. It was defined as interest, motivation, commitment to the profession and hard work. Effort may be expressed in a variety of ways. For example, the punctual submission of assignments, attendance and enthusiasm for the subject or work setting. Effort may be linked with professional suitability. For example, 'Effort is double-edged. If a borderline student has been inconsistent, sloppy and late then we ask 'How are they going to be as a practitioner?'' (manager). In attributional theory, effort is an internal, unstable and controllable causal factor for success or failure in achievement-related situations. Effort was valued, particularly by work-based assessors, who admitted wishing to reward 'hard work' even though the student had not achieved the outcomes. This was especially the case in the early stage of courses. The tendency to encourage and support first year students, to reward their motivation rather than skills has also been noted in nursing (Bradley, 1990).

Differentiating between a borderline fail and a borderline pass, although difficult, seems to depend upon individual or collective perceptions about potential and effort. These are subtle, subjective criteria. They need to be based upon sound assessment principles. This is to prevent abuse for it is as unjust to fail a student who should pass as it is to pass one who should fail.

Borderline performance to be failed

The next two factors are different, one being counter-intuitive and the other relating to external pressures. First, students sometime deliberately perform at borderline level. A work-practice organiser gave two examples which illustrate two contrasting motivations. 'She felt it was OK to fail a work placement rather than be labelled academically unsuitable. The other was only interested in gaining paper qualifications. They both wanted the system to fail them so they could do what they really wanted. The second student did just enough to pass. This made the supervisor angry because she knew the student had the potential to do better.' These highlight the need to understand the student's perspective.

Overall percentage of marks

The second factor – the overall percentage marks for individuals and the cohort – is an external pressure which can add to the complexity of a fail scenario. It comprises the flexibility of an individuals' mark and the flexibility of the pass grade. The collation of the marks from all assessments at the end of a semester or academic level or year is more than a mathematical exercise. It involves judgement. These may be influenced by past performance and staff expectations. For example, 'on a small course you know the students well. You feel let down if one you expect to pass, fails. If it is borderline, they get a pass' (manager). There is also flexibility in marks given to the cohort – the whole group. An inexperienced lecturer described the 'arbitrary way of allocating percentages. I was amazed how the goal posts move. For example, when the marks are raised for the whole group if there are lots of fails, so more pass.' Recently, the Thames Valley University was pilloried in *The Sunday Times* for 'dumbing down its degrees' (26 October 1997). The report described how the 'university effectively dropped the pass mark from 40 per cent to 30 per cent and permitted students to fail almost half their courses over a year but continue their degrees … account [had been taken of] exceptional circumstances and [we] allowed anyone who had a mark of 30 per cent at their resit to be condoned as passing.' Marks may also be decreased as well as increased. This is likely to provoke official complaints and academic appeals from students, especially if the confirmed grade jeopardises final degree classifications (Utley, 1997).

The generality or global nature of the criteria for assigning a fail grade is striking especially when compared with the detailed specifications for occupational standards and National Vocational Qualifications. Interestingly though, research into very different employment sectors (Engineering, Construction and Administration) indicates assessors, internal and external verifiers still use personal, global or employer-specific criteria. These implicit, internalised models of competence seem to take precedence over the prescribed, official criteria (Eraut et al., 1996).

Incompetence

This is another elusive concept. The dictionary defines incompetent as 'not qualified or able to perform a particular task or function, showing a lack of skill'. In this context it is associated with unsafe and unscrupulous behaviour for these terms encompass the problems of performance and conduct. These are outlined in this section to illustrate the 'neat fit' between the criteria for failure, definitions of incompetence and competence.

Incompetence has received scant attention in literature of the 'caring professions'. This may be related to the 'norm of non-criticism…the conspiracy of tolerance' which Rosenthal (1995, p. 125) states is part of medical culture. This is changing with the spread of audit, complaints procedures and statutory regulations. The study of errors, mistakes and adverse events is more advanced in other sectors such as aviation where they are used to prevent recurrence. Medical errors have been categorised in different ways. For example:

- errors of implementation (problems occur when utilising what is known)
- errors of ignorance (not having the necessary knowledge to carry out particular clinical procedures).

Another categorisation is normative lapses (breaches in the accepted codes of behaviour) and technical mistakes (failures in skills and procedures). Allsop and Mulchay (1996) note 'the problem of identification of poor practice (in medical work) is only a starting point' (p. 31). They list six issues:

- inexperience
- work pressure
- interpersonal or personality problems
- age and impairment
- lack of knowledge or skill
- criminal behaviour.

This list illustrates the interaction between the person and their environment. Also, the lack of an absolute standard of performance. In Rosenthal's (1995) study of 'the incompetent doctor' she defined problems as

- impaired doctors by virtue of substance abuse, physical illness, mental illness or manifestations of ageing
- doctors whose knowledge or skills are poor by the standards of their peers
- doctors who are "burnt-out", over-worked or having personal problems
- doctors whose personalities and personal behaviour are seen as problematic in the work environment
- doctors who may be having a "run" of bad results.' (p. 8)

She proposes a general definition of incompetence which 'includes consistent, demonstrated lack of knowledge and/or skills in the conduct of clinical practice, and the production of below-standard outcomes' (p. 8). It is still broad, although less ambiguous. This is because it is difficult, if not impossible, to identify specific markers on the continuum of competence–incompetence. However, there are some general, recurring criteria.

These include grossness and frequency of error, lack of insight and ability to learn from a mistake and quality of interpersonal relationships. The latter figured in Donaldson's research on the problems of senior hospital doctors (1994). In order of frequency, these were

- poor attitude and disruptive or irresponsible behaviour
- lack of commitment to duties
- badly exercised clinical skills and inadequate medical knowledge
- dishonesty
- sexual overtones in dealing with patients or staff or both
- disorganised practise
- poor communication with colleagues.

Although all these examples are from the medical profession, the definitions are sufficiently broad (and pertinent) to be generalisable to other professions. Interestingly, all these definitions mirror an American study conducted by Gutman, McCreedy and Heisler (1998) investigating the reasons why students who performed well academically failed work placements. A review of records between 1986–1995 revealed eight communicative and behavioural characteristics for failure in professional settings. The reasons were attributed to emotional, rather than academic intelligence, and comprised rigidity of thinking, discomfort with the ambiguity that accompanies clinical reasoning, lack of psychological insight, difficulty interpreting feedback, externalisation of responsibility, difficulty learning from mistakes, discomfort with the physical handling of patients, and dependence on external measures for self-esteem.

Competence

Last, but certainly not least, we consider competence. There are many ways for determining entry level competency, including observation, job and task analysis, critical incident analysis, behavioural event interviews, Delphi and nominal group techniques. These different methods have produced remarkably similar results in a range of health care professions. Some examples are presented in Table 2.4. This contains profession-specific and shared knowledge and skills. The commonalties relate to the treatment or problem-solving process, interpersonal and written communication with clients and colleagues, management of self, and the service, legal and ethical requirements linked to professional values, attitudes and codes of conduct. They are the obverse of incompetence and the criteria for failure.

The maintenance of entry level knowledge and skills is the minimum requirement for continued competence. There is an expectation of progression through keeping up-to-date with information, technological developments, changes in the policy environment and through the use of research evidence about the effectiveness of practice. Continued competence builds

Table 2.4 International comparison of the expectations of entry level competence in some health and social care professions over the last two decades (Direct comparison is unwise as the statements were obtained by different methods and for different purposes. For example, those for nursing relate to 'practical nursing skills' while the expectations for social work are core assessment criteria.)

Expectations	Nursing	Physiotherapy	Nutritionists	Medicine	Social work
Assessment					
Assessment skills	✓	✓			
Perform screening			✓		
Organ system examination			✓	✓	
Interpret scientific data					
Intellectual flexibility				✓	
Problem definition – hypothesis generation			✓	✓	✓
Planning					
Planning skills	✓				
Programme planning		✓	✓		
Implementation					
Executive effectiveness	✓				✓
Implementation skills	✓				
Nutrition services to community health programmes			✓		
Safe implementation		✓			
Clinical and diagnostic procedures			✓	✓	
Prepare educational materials					
Evaluation skills	✓				
Interpersonal skills					
Effective communication				✓	
Patient interviewing – screening examination					✓

(contd)

Table 2.4 (contd)

Expectations	Nursing	Physiotherapy	Nutritionists	Medicine	Social work
Professional and interpersonal skills					
Communication	✓		✓		
Interpersonal effectiveness		✓			✓
Motivational skills		✓			
Counselling			✓		
Empathy			✓		
Communicate in teaching			✓		
Multidisciplinary team work		✓		✓	
Collaboration – communication with colleagues					
Management					
Consultative and administrative capacities	✓	✓	✓		
Management skills			✓		
Food service management			✓		
Programme administration			✓		
Legislative activism			✓		
Consumer advocate			✓		
Supervisor paraprofessionals			✓		
Long-term service planning			✓		
Mass media communication					
In-service education					
Ethical, professional behaviour					
Ethical and legal requirements		✓			
Legal, ethical and value concerns				✓	✓
Commitment to professional values					

Table 2.4 (contd)

Expectations	Nursing	Physiotherapy	Nutritionists	Medicine	Social work
Personal attitudes to professional life					
Continuous professional learning		√			√
Knowledge					
Maintaining currency within the discipline				√	
Effective synthesis of a wide range of knowledge					√

References:

Nursing: United Kingdom. Aggleton P, Allen M and Montgomery S (1987) Developing a system for the continuous assessment of practical nursing skills. Nurse Education Today, 7, pp.158–64.

Physiotherapy: South Africa. Beenhakker J C (1987) Determinants of Physiotherapy Education. Medical Teacher, 9, 2, pp.161–65.

Nutritionists: United States of America. Sims L S (1979) Identification and evaluation of competencies of Public Health Nutritionists. AJPH, 69, 11, pp.1099–1105.

Medicine: United States of America and Canada. Scott C S, Barrows H S, Brock D M and Hunt D D. (1991) Clinical behaviours and skills that faculty form 12 institutions judged were essential for medical students to acquire. Academic Medicine, 66, 2, pp.106–11.

Social work: United Kingdom. Maisch M and Winter R (1991) The ASSET Programme. Volume 2 The Development and Assessment of Professional Competences. Anglia Polytechnic University and Essex County Council Social Services.

upon the common core of professional expertise, but becomes differenti-ated, more specialised and context specific. Table 2.5 contains the generic competencies of senior house officers identified during a research project conducted in the Northern and Yorkshire Region of the United Kingdom (Ilott and Allen, 1997). These make explicit the expectations of this first grade of registered medical practitioners. The taxonomy of clinical, managerial, supervisory, personal and professional development (particu-larly the last three categories) is also shared by other professions. Most importantly, conduct and ethical expectations are embedded within the core to reflect the standards of service delivery demanded by the National Health Service.

Table 2.5 Core competencies of senior house officers

The competencies were identified during research conducted within Northern and Yorkshire Region between February 1995 and April 1996. The study was jointly funded by the National Health Service Executive and Department for Education and Employment. The clinical, managerial, supervisory and developmental roles with their constituents provided the framework for a continuum of integrated competence. This specifies progression from entry level, through general professional/basic specialist training, to exit statements as prerequisites for higher specialist training in six acute disciplines. The revised version of the core competencies incorporate changes following feedback from the dissemination phase. These changes are in italics. All doctors are expected to meet the standards of competence, care and conduct outlined in *Good Medical Practice* (GMC, 1995).

Purpose: A senior house officer is to learn to be a safe, medical practitioner developing clinical acumen, problem solving and independent decision-making competencies necessary for sound, professional judgements and timely action. This is gained through the process of providing front line health care and reviewing the outcome with more experienced doctors.

Clinical role: Responsible for the admission, initial assessment and management of acute, emergency and elective admissions.

1. Apply sufficient knowledge and skill in the diagnostic process to ensure safe practice.
2. Recognise the limits of own competence, willing to seek and accept assistance from medical or non-medical colleagues.
3. *Establish a professional, patient–doctor relationship based upon trust, respect and an empathetic understanding of the concerns of the patients and their relatives.*
4. Establish differential and probable diagnosis for patients presenting with acute and common conditions encountered in current specialty.
5. Obtain a diagnosis from properly tailored, relevant history taking, specific examina-tions and specialised investigations appropriate to each individual patient.
6. Contribute to the decision making, organisation, interpretation and ongoing review of diagnostic investigations or treatment interventions.
7. Contribute to decision making about acute and non-acute management plans which incorporate contingency planning and review for patients presenting with common conditions.

Table 2.5 (contd)

8. Develop management of the 'whole patient' including health promotion, disease prevention and long-term management plans.
9. Employ appropriate consulting skills to elicit the history, inform, explain or clarify the diagnosis and treatment options for patients presenting with common conditions in current specialty.
10. Assist at clinics, contributing to the assessment, monitoring, review and discharge of follow-up patients or new patients attending for a single consultation.
11. Contribute to effective discharge with the medical, multiprofessional team and patient related to decision making, organisation and documentation including follow-up with primary or community care agencies.
12. Adopt a critical, questioning approach to anecdotal or evidence-based medicine through audit and an appreciation of the 'art of medicine'.
13. *Observe the profession's ethical obligations by respecting patients' rights, dignity, privacy and confidentiality.*

Managerial role: Responsible for the management of own workload whilst being a junior, equal member and leader in different teams at different times.

1. Organise time and medical tasks efficiently during structured sessions (clinics, ward rounds, theatre), when on call *and arranging cover.*
2. Manage simultaneous tasks, setting and changing priorities for individual patients and the whole caseload *based upon principles of equality and ethical resource management.*
3. Establish effective working relationships with members of ward, departmental, interdisciplinary and multiprofessional or other teams in primary, secondary and community care including making appropriate referrals and receiving reports.
4. Accept advice from, make decisions with and learn from more experienced non-medical team members without relinquishing responsibility.
5. Accept leadership role as the ward doctor especially during medical emergencies taking charge in a calm, decisive manner.
6. Negotiate different roles with medical colleagues which includes establishing relationships with senior doctors when acting as a patient's advocate when referring up or to other specialties.
7. Present salient information collated from relevant sources succinctly in oral and written forms, *keeping accurate patient records.*

Supervisory role: Contribute to the support, supervision and teaching of PRHOs, medical students and other staff.

1. Delegate, monitor and regularly review the work of house officers whether attached to ward, department or when on call following initial assessment of confidence and capabilities.
2. Be approachable and willing to provide advice or information, sharing experiences and questioning to promote learning of self and others.
3. Teach, demonstrate and provide assistance with difficult instances of basic practical procedures.
4. Respond to others' needs for professional and emotional support through peer support on a formal or informal basis for less experienced/other doctors.

(contd)

Table 2.5 (contd)

Developmental role: Optimise formal and informal learning opportunities for professional and personal development.

1. Consolidate and extend clinical competency and confidence from registration.
2. Obtain general and professional experience to assist career choice or fulfil career plan with forward planning to encompass next stage/s.
3. Embark on basic specialist training to support preparation for membership/fellowship examinations by gaining sufficient exposure to range of specialty and some sub-specialties.
4. Achieve higher degree/qualification.
5. Develop generic skills to support effective contribution within health care organisations, for example computer literacy, corporate responsibility, *management of conflict and complaints*, 'political awareness', and networking.
6. Maintain own health and well being through a balance between vocational commitment and over commitment.
7. Promote life-long learning, using skills of self-directed learning to keep abreast of developments and contributing to a learning culture through topic or case presentations, offering new ideas and good practices from other posts.

November 1996

Conclusion: using the unspoken consensus to assist examiners

Interestingly, it is easier to articulate the criteria for assigning a fail grade, to identify the constituents of incompetence, than to define competence. This approach avoids the semantic confusion and conflict between the different definitions of competence or capability. Competence is an elusive concept, especially when one tries to link it to very specific assessment criteria. Perhaps this is appropriate because 'practice...depends on a subtle blend of values, attitudes, knowledge and skills; and on the capacity for making flexible responses to an infinite variety of situations, many of which cannot be anticipated (Brandon and Davies, 1979, p. 299). This quotation mirrors the definition of higher level, National Vocational Qualifications (Mitchell, 1993). Such a global definition, with a sound foundation in the constants of professional, ethical behaviour, allows flexibility in the context of skills mix with the blurring of roles and responsibilities between different professions.

There is nothing new about the observation that assessors and examiners working in a wide variety of educational settings have to make complex judgements (Murphy, 1994; Murphy and Joyes, 1996). It is rarely possible, in the realm of education, to describe assessment criteria with a high level of specificity. As Gipps (1994) and others have pointed out, 'assessment is not an exact science, and we must stop pretending it is such. This is of course part of the post-modern condition – a suspension of belief in the absolute status of "scientific knowledge"...The constructionist paradigm does not accept that reality is fixed and independent of the observer; rather reality is constructed by the observer, thus there are multiple constructions of reality' (p. 167). Thus assessment of educational achievements is blighted both by the complexity of the nature of these achievements and the philosophical challenge of reconciling the observations of one individual with that of others. To a certain degree any assessment of professional competence is dependent upon who is making that judgement, when and where. Upholding professional standards, however, requires that variations in individual judgements are kept to a very small area of uncertainty, otherwise we are left without any confidence at all in the concept of their being 'professional standards.'

A global conceptualisation may be a heretical suggestion as explicit standards and outcomes dominate the competency movement. But, academic and work-based assessors can balance objective and subjective evidence 'intuitive and analytic thinking...to grasp the situation as a whole' (Blomquist, 1985, p. 9). This ability may be grounded in an unspoken consensus about what constitutes incompetence. It seems to be enhanced by clarifying and comparing criteria, reviewing the use and misuse of implicit or explicit constructs with intra and interprofessional colleagues (Ilott, 1995). The reassurance gained from recognising similar criteria and threshold standards affirms their expert role by confirming both the validity and inter-rater reliability (Friedman and Mennin, 1991) of their judgements.

This book is intended to support examiners by preparing them for the potential trauma of assigning a fail grade. All assessors must fulfil their obligation to protect the public and minimise the number of 'horror stories'. This obligation stems from the privilege of professional self-regulation. A conspiracy of silence cannot be justified. But such exhortations are easy. The next chapter will explore the complex constellation of reasons why these exhortations are sometimes ignored and the award of a fail grade is avoided.

Chapter 3
Why it is difficult to fail students

Introduction: A multifaceted model

Each fail scenario has a unique set of consequences and circumstances. Indeed every 'borderline' case is a potential failure, and those working in professional education are frequently dealing with borderline students (Fraser et al., 1997). Here a multifaceted model is presented to help assessors understand the internal and external factors which could influence their decision making in such situations. Understanding why failure is difficult may prevent the most undesirable outcomes of assessment. These range from costly student appeals to allowing incompetent practitioners to progress whether at entry or post-qualification levels. The model attempts to outline the factors which can operate at individual, institutional and external levels. It was derived from a synthesis of international, inter-disciplinary literature and the wisdom accumulated from a group of experienced assessors during a series of focused interviews.

The model presents the three interdependent elements of individual characteristics, institutional contexts and external pressures which influence the judgement of 'competence to practise'. Each of the three elements contains different facets such as negative and positive points, personal and cultural aspects. The elements impinge in varying ways depending upon the circumstances and consequences of the fail grade. This chapter aims to disentangle the complex combination of subtle, but powerful pressures which may distort judgements.

Judgements at the margins of competency in professional training can be troublesome. One reason is the difficulty of defining and then assessing 'competence to practise'. Meta-analysis of tools to assess clinical competency criticise their lack of rigor, validity and reliability in a range of professions including nursing (Coates and Chambers 1992) and occupational therapy (Barker, 1990). In medicine Jolly, Wakeford and Newble (1994) note that 'many current assessment practices have detrimental effects on the person being assessed...assessment is often too cursory to make very much sense of the result' (p. 231). These technical difficulties may be compounded by the affective aspects of assigning a fail grade. It can be a work stress. 'Working with failing students' and 'failing clinically unsafe students' were rated as the second and third highest occupational stressors by Goldenberg and Waddall (1990). Other 'unfortunate outcomes [are] ...burnout, loss of high calibre clinical faculty members' (Symanski, 1991, p. 18).

Yet, such decisions are intrinsic to the role of 'teacher-as-judge'. It is important to be aware of the multifactorial reasons why it can constitute a work stress. Awareness is the prerequisite for understanding and change. Awareness incorporates confronting the fail taboo and recognising the benefits, as well as costs, in acting to protect the public. The model presents some reasons for the stress levels related to the individual (both staff and student), the external pressures which exert an influence on the assessor and the institutional context.

Individual characteristics of assessor and student

The first element of individual factors encompasses characteristics of the assessor and student. Some are positive, some are negative and there may be a reciprocal influence of one factor upon both individuals. There are many facets within this element. This section alerts the reader to the variation which makes each fail dynamic and unique.

Characteristics of the assessor

Direct responsibility adds to the difficulty

It seems that staff with direct responsibility for making pass–fail decisions are likely to experience the greatest level of stress even though such results are usually a collective judgement. In most academic settings decision making is shared with internal and external examiners. Assessors in practice settings, including those working single-handedly, also use others to corroborate or contradict their concerns. Second opinions may be gained formally or informally from peers and members of the interdisciplinary team, line managers and work-practice organisers from the academic establishment. Regardless of setting, such support networks seem to be essential even though they do not diminish the assessor's sense of individual responsibility. A supervisor described how the decision was 'mine, with supervision from the line manger. But ultimately it was me who said pass or fail'.

Affective reactions

The feelings provoked by failing and coping with the spread of emotional turbulence is one of the key reasons why failing is difficult. The next chapter is devoted to this but some of the pertinent fears and feelings are outlined here. Metaphors convey the depth and range of some of these feelings. For example, 'I was tearing my hair out' (supervisor), 'I was emotionally drained – wrung out' (lecturer). They encompass fear, self-interrogation, guilt, anger, anxiety and 'sense of failure if you have put a lot of effort to stop them failing the retake. We do not want students to fail, we feel failures ourselves' (lecturer).

Such feelings explain why students are sometimes allowed to 'just pass' as this avoids the trauma associated with difficult decision making. The tendency to 'pass the buck' has been reported in such diverse professions as social work (Brandon and Davies, 1979) and medicine (Green, 1991). A work-based supervisor outlined the process: 'You find reasons to push them through. For example, you've been ill or you blame yourself for not giving them enough time.' This failure to fail may not always be welcomed by the student. For example, one reacted by saying she thought she should have failed. The supervisor who had 'just passed her' agreed with the student's self-evaluation. The reasons for this act of 'professional cowardice' (Lankshear, 1990) were discussed in Chapter 2.

Failing is especially difficult for inexperienced staff

Failing can be even more traumatic for inexperienced staff. Inexperience spans newness to practise and to the role of assessor. Newly qualified practitioners are vulnerable to identification as they negotiate the transition from assessed to assessor (Kremer-Hayon, 1986). Some professions stipulate a one-year period before practitioners are allowed to supervise students in work settings. New assessors also lack a reference level of comparative experience about baseline standards or expectations at each stage and the end of training. Differentiating between learning time and learning potential, accommodating individual variations is another challenge. Practice with the opportunity to learn through trial and error without assessment anxiety is part of the learning process. This requires fine judgements about learning and assessment time. Inexperienced examiners are also likely to be less familiar with, and perhaps more fearful of, misinterpreting assessment regulations and appeals procedures. Identification can also affect experienced, work-based assessors. 'It was difficult for my colleague. She had failed a work placement. All her bad memories came flooding back. These increased her distress. She was going through what the student was going through.'

Inexperience may be due to lack of opportunity. The failure of students is rare in work-based settings. A supervisor dealing with individual students does not have the reassurance of comparing that student with a large annual cohort. In a typical cohort, even one as exceptional as students in higher education, or professionals undertaking post-qualification training, a bell-shaped distribution curve may be seen to presuppose some fails – although with the trend toward competence-based assessments this may not necessarily be the case. The assessment of competence to practise is complex. It is unsurprising that inexperienced assessors may lack confidence and be reluctant to assign a fail grade.

The closer the relationship the more difficult failing can be

The closeness of the relationship can increase or decrease the degree of difficulty experienced by staff. Tutors and supervisors are most likely to know the student as an individual, not just a face in the crowd, even in mass higher education. Also in the so-called 'caring professions' the tutors' own training may have taught them to feel some responsibility to do all in their power to achieve a positive outcome for the person (student) in their care. This knowledge of personal circumstances and foibles can cause most regret when a hard-working, motivated, well-known or liked student fails. Faulty attributions and subjectivity may influence decision making, especially when effort, not the achievement of minimum standards, is rewarded. There can be sadness when the fail is attributed to lack of ability rather than effort – the student has worked hard, responded to feedback and improved a little but not enough. A special, collusive relationship may develop between staff and student with the provision of extraordinary amounts of help to secure a pass grade. The assessor may be reluctant to give candid formative and summative feedback and therefore award a luke-warm pass grade (Bradley, 1990) .

The relationship between a personal tutor–tutee and supervisor– student share certain characteristics. Both are one-to-one for an extended period of time. It allows progress and problems to be monitored. This causes dilemmas which can lead to conflict between academic and pastoral roles, especially when the pastoral role takes precedence. The member of staff may become too involved and be unduly influenced by the student's personal problems. Alternatively, it may be because a personal tutee has not asked for help from the personal tutor. The resultant guilt was described as 'it was my responsibility to have known, done or helped more'. The increasing demands upon academic staff, whether from the research assessment exercises or income generation, may create anxiety due to insufficient time or training to fulfil this role. However, there are benefits from the insights which comes from a closer relationship. This was described by a lecturer: 'You have an honest relationship with them. This means you are able to give the reasons more clearly, explore alternatives. There is more dignity.'

The closeness of the relationship may exacerbate feelings of guilt, personal responsibility and self-interrogation. The conflict between educator and pastoral roles add to the complexity. Some of the problems within the apprenticeship model of supervision (and pastoral support) are noted by Boydell: 'It seems rather hypocritical and dishonest for a supervisor to engage a [student] in collaborative work and interpersonal effort and then to 'fail' that [student] if those efforts don't pan out productively'(1986, p. 122). The apprenticeship model is at the heart of work-based learning, reflective practice and service-based learning for many health and social care professions. It is based upon the assumption that professional practice is best learned through time-served observing, working alongside and imitating a 'master practitioner'. Recently, in other areas such as the preparation of school teachers and probation officers, there have been moves to reposition training back into more of an apprenticeship mode. Some would say this move has been motivated by fear of the type of influence higher education experiences may have upon students being prepared for these professions.

Student characteristics

It is a truism to state that each student is an individual while sharing certain characteristics with other students. Personal characteristics include gender, age and ethnicity. Other commonalties relate to the academic route, assessment setting and relationship with the assessor. Examiners may be influenced by knowing the identities, race and sex of the students (Gipps and Murphy, 1994; Partington, Brown and Gordon, 1993). Common dimensions derived from the academic route include the level of programme, whether it is studied on a part-time or full-time basis and the year of training. The setting – academic or work – influences the intimacy of the relationship, whether one-to-one work-based supervision or a pastoral relationship as a personal tutor–tutee. Although presented separately each facet can interact with another, especially gender and age.

Sexual harassment and bias

Prohibition may ban but cannot eliminate sexual relationships between students and staff. Lecturers are required by codes of conduct and sexual harassment policies to maintain a professional distance and boundaries. Personal, particularly sexual relationships with students compromise their integrity and are likely to be exploitative due to the imbalance of power. Nevertheless, gender pervades all human relationships (Lips, 1991). This ranges from sexual identity, through sexual attraction to sex role stereotypes. The gender of the student and staff exert what may simply be seen as a subliminal influence. A male lecturer commented upon the positive and negative impact of sexual attraction: 'If I am attracted to a female student it is more difficult to be objective and fail her. Sometimes a student may play temptress to help her pass. If I suspect a student is a homosexual, I may be less objective – it is easier to fail.'

The 'caring' professions, with the exception of medicine, tend to be female-dominated with the minority of men in senior management posts. There may be positive or negative discrimination against male students who are performing at the margins of competence. These may be expressed in entrenched attitudes toward male students who are deemed unsuitable or unable to cope. Alternatively, they may be 'given the benefit of the doubt'. A female lecturer reported sadness because 'we need men in the profession and for the atmosphere of the whole group'. A male student's response may confirm or contradict the sex role stereotypes held by the assessor. An aggressive blaming response, although predicted, was difficult for a female examiner who disliked conflict. A tearful response was equally difficult for another who said 'when a male student cried, I was shocked and surprised'.

Mature, male students

In some professions, such as occupational therapy, males tend to be mature students. The combination of age and gender seems to exert a different influence. Older, male students may expect younger, female supervisors to misunderstand them. Younger, female staff may be intimidated by assertive mature, male students. Older, male students may retaliate with sex role stereotypes, for example: 'but I have a wife and kids to support. I'll be unemployable and you can't do this to me.'

Mature students and school leavers

Initiatives to widen access for non-traditional students and those with non-standard entry qualifications has resulted in mature students outnumbering school leavers within some parts of higher education in the UK. Failing mature students seems to be particularly difficult because 'it is more tragic for them' (lecturer). There are many reasons. Staff recognise the investment and personal sacrifices for a mature student and their family. They tend to be more committed, having made a careful career choice. Mature students are seen as hard working, highly motivated and enthusiastic. These internal, controllable factors are valued by teachers and resulted in sadness when failure is attributed to lack of ability rather than effort (Graham, 1984). Mature students may also be more disappointed, taking longer to adjust because of 'higher expectations of themselves. They have difficulties working with and taking criticism from younger supervisors, especially if these relate to interpersonal skills.'

School leavers' withdrawals were viewed as less traumatic because they had more time and potential to change career direction. This is not to deny their distress which may be attributed to their immaturity, vulnerability and threat to their self-esteem which increases with age 'more noticeably after adolescence' (Dell and Valine, 1990, p. 159). Also, the parental reactions to failure 'for eighteen year olds the pressure is from others. Parents can be troublesome' (manager).

Ethnicity

The student population reflects the multicultural, multiethnic society in the United Kingdom. Some are from first, second or third generation ethnic minority families while others are international students. For example, in the academic year 1996–97 the latter comprised 12 per cent (n = 198,400) of the population at UK higher education colleges and universities. Most overseas students (22.3 per cent) are postgraduates with 8.2 per cent on first degree programmes. Just as codes of conduct cannot eliminate sexual dynamics, so legislation and equal opportunities policies cannot eliminate racism or accusations of racial bias or harassment. International students obtain a higher percentage of first class honours (8.1 per cent) compared with all entrants (6.9 per cent). However, a much higher percentage of international students are awarded third class honours, almost twice the proportion of all first degree students (Nye, 1997). Third class and pass degrees are generally considered 'not satisfactory' (Charter, 1997) i.e. to represent a failure to fail.

The judgements of assessors may be influenced by other factors such as an understanding of different cultural reactions to failure with 'loss of face' or the expectation of multiple retakes as permitted in some European Union countries. The career of post-registration students in their home countries may be tainted for many years by failure. A prime example is overseas doctors who do not gain membership of a Medical Royal College during their period of residence in the UK. Another influence is the pressure to be lenient and set a different threshold standard for pre-registration students undertaking professional training. International students may carry the extra responsibility of self, parental or government sponsorship to develop services in their country of origin on completion. Although they may not attain minimum standards for the UK, their performance may be judged acceptable for a developing country and service. The dilemma is that a pass grade confers the opportunity to register and work anywhere (in the UK and eligibility to apply to other countries such as the USA, Canada, Australia and New Zealand) and not just their home country. A similar pressure may apply to second and third generation UK immigrants where there is a desire to widen access to professional education so as to provide a more culturally sensitive service to ethnic groups.

Difficulties due to differences in academic routes

The last decade has seen many changes in the education of health and social care professions. Many vocational programmes have become part of higher education institutions. There is co-terminosity of higher diplomas or honours degrees with registration which enhances the academic status of practice-based professions. There has been a corresponding expansion in higher degrees for continued professional development.

Diversity and devolvement of control to local level are common features of the changes. There is diversity in curricula, mode of delivery and students. Core curricula, syllabi or guidelines set by professional or statutory bodies may be interpreted by each higher education institution.

Programmes are delivered via full- or part-time routes extending for two-, three- or four-year periods depending upon the experience or entry qualifications of the cohort. Students are also more heterogeneous with the traditional, 18-year-old school leaver often in the minority.

Changes in academic status and course content can create tensions within essentially practical professions. These often focus upon the maintenance of professional standards, concerns about the gap between theory and practice and the need to ensure practitioners fit the criteria of fitness to practise and for purpose as well as award. Nevertheless, assessors are still required to judge competence to practise.

Perceptions of any difference between failing a student studying a diploma or a degree course in occupational therapy revealed two issues. First, the degree had been designed so weak students could 'be weeded out at the end of the first year' (manager). Assessment regulations were written to enable 'failure to be confronted earlier' (lecturer). Second, degree students were expected to be more questioning, articulate and challenging. They were seen to be 'more anxious about their assessments especially how the grade effects their honours classification' (lecturer). Some supervisors admitted feeling intimidated by degree students, particularly when they used terminology which highlighted the gap between theoretical approaches and everyday practice. Academic staff referred to the pressure to achieve academic standards 'as an indication of our abilities'. This tendency toward a causal theory of teaching was balanced by a desire to maintain professional standards: 'we need to be confident enough to fail' (manager).

There are now many different routes for professional training. These include accelerated, two-year programmes for graduates, four-year, in-service courses for support workers and distance, open learning courses. Each route may create extra and different difficulties. Graduate students may be perceived to be disadvantaged by the accelerated pace of learning which hinders integration and professional socialisation. They may be subject to even higher academic expectations but with the assumption of poor practical or interpersonal skills. The reluctance to fail part-time, in-service students was linked to their employee status as support workers and as a mature student. There were fears about the attitudes of employers toward the 'student returning to work as a failure' having not gained the expected return on their investment of time and money.

Timing is everything: failing in the first, second and final year

The timing of a fail grade illustrates the reciprocal influence of one facet upon both student and assessor. The language used to describe a first year or final year fail is very different. For example, academic staff tend to expect marginal students 'to be weeded out' or 'sifted out' during the first year. These metaphors reflect a process of differentiation for the common good. The student is open to alternatives. The action is a relief, 'a kindness to save further pain for the student and staff'. Termination of training at a mid-way point was more acceptable especially if the student 'had been given the benefit of the doubt in year one'. The repetition of problems (having received extra time and help to develop) seemed to be reassuring for it confirmed withdrawal as the appropriate outcome.

In contrast, a final year fail was considered unforgivable because 'it is morally unethical to allow a student to reach this stage'. It provoked anger and distress: 'it was very traumatic, the worst thing that has happened to me in teaching'. There was individual and collective guilt for the waste of time, money, effort and a scarce training place. 'Nobody has an excuse and can be excused.' Lecturers offered three reasons why a final year fail was the worst:

- First, self-blame, guilt and responsibility for allowing a student to reach this stage, especially if there was a history of marginal performance. It represented a failure of individuals and the system.
- Second, there was the totality of the waste of time and investment. 'It is very difficult because a fail may effect their job, mortgage and marriage.'
- Finally, the implications of failing at the point when their career aspirations had become a virtual reality. Some students had obtained employment.

Such pressures highlight the need for courage. It may explain why final year fails are relatively rare 'in the British system, [and the] widespread reluctance to fail a candidate who has reached the end of a course' (Warren-Piper, 1994, p. 178).

Although work-based assessors seem to experience all fails as equally traumatic, they also adopt a more pragmatic approach to a final year fail. This was due to the student's proximity to licence and liberty to practise. 'If you allow them to pass, then they will soon be qualified. You need to ask whether you would want them to treat your parents.' It was still hard because 'there is something deep and fundamentally difficult about failing on the last placement. It cost me dear in emotional upheaval. Everyone expected her to scrape through because she was due to qualify in a few weeks. It would have been much easier to do this but I would have been justified in failing her at any time. She was unreliable. She was accusatory and attempted emotional blackmail. It was very tough.'

The final year should be the most challenging academically and professionally. This is the basis for the incremental, developmental approach to academic 'levels' which underpin diploma or degree programmes. Students in their last work placement are expected to perform as entry grade practitioners (Cohn and Frum, 1988). A stage approach, which usually accommodates the possibility of plateau or peaking at an earlier stage, may explain the occurrence of final year fails. Another reason relates to prevention. This is because such judgements are better made at an earlier, easier and less wasteful stage of the educational programme. These dilemmas were neatly summarised by Brandon and Davies nearly two decades ago: 'there is an impression of difficult decisions postponed by avoidance, which are then all the harder to take at a later stage because of the investment of time by student and teachers, and of scarce resources by course and placement agency...once the decision is postponed to the second year, the pressure towards granting an automatic pass becomes almost irresistible' (1979, p. 338).

Failure is more difficult the second time around

The consequences of a first and final fail are of a different order of magnitude. A first fail is redeemable. It can be positive in that 'it can spur them on. It gives them a shock to sort themselves out' (lecturer). Students are given the opportunity to consolidate their learning, to improve and demonstrate their commitment to the course. It is a safety net for those who 'might just pass, they gain extra time, concentrating on one paper can lead to amazing differences in quality' (manager). Failing can be part of learning and not necessarily a disaster. Some managers commented that a first fail should be 'definite, not a 39 per cent with a pass mark of 40 per cent'. This was to convey the 'right message' as they did not wish the fail grade to be misinterpreted as a near miss, an apology or a sign of misplaced kindness.

Many examination regulations require withdrawal from the course following failure on a retake assessment. This can mean termination of training. It is this outcome which provokes the affective response summarised by a lecturer as 'when a student fails early in the course there is a lot of anger, especially if they leave immediately or reject help. If you help them, push them through but they still fail the resit, then it is the student who feels angry, guilty and responsible. Staff are absolved because they have satisfied their own need to care for the student or compensate for their guilt.' The process must be fair and appropriate. An assessor reported taking 'even more care to ensure my decision is valid' asking colleagues to double and triple mark assessment. Much deliberation can occur within the whole or a sub-set of the staff group. Many factors may be taken into consideration during the decision making including:

- the student's whole profile of performance and potential
- whether they 'deserved to fail'
- their attendance and professional behaviour exhibited in the academic setting
- whether there are grounds for an appeal.

These factors illustrate some of the advantages and disadvantages of small cohorts. 'Students are well known...there are personal dynamics. We want to be fair and not stereotype them as problems' (lecturer). However, these factors are implicit assessment constructs (Rowntree, 1987) which seem to be negotiable and are negotiated during such discussions.

External influences upon the assessor

A mix of two factors seem to influence an assessor's judgement. The first is humanistic principles which can create a fundamental tension between educator and therapist roles and values. This tension is classified as an external influence because it arises from the subtle process of professional socialisation. The value system is so integral as to be almost invisible. The second factor – the causal theory of teaching – is equally subtle and pervasive. This exerts a powerful influence upon individuals and institutions.

Humanistic principles a fundamental cause of difficulty

Humanistic values underpin the preparation of practitioners for many education, health and social care professions. The humanistic values and roles of an educator and therapist may be perceived as complementary, particularly when facilitating student-directed learning or client-centred work. Conflict can arise when the boundaries become blurred, when the process interferes with the outcome. This danger was exemplified by a lecturer: 'They become a hindrance when you give the student extra time, the benefit of the doubt so they can reach their potential. We need to remember they must be competent...in an emergency they could be dealing with our relatives.' When humanistic values and roles collide there can be a deep rooted conflict which explains why fails are so stressful. Values are perceptions of desirable behaviour related to one's professional identity and activities. These perceptions about what is intrinsically good are operationalised as a set of humanistic values and expressed in roles. It is this fundamental linkage which can create role strain for assessors. Humanity is the simple, common core of humanistic values. It comprises assumptions about the nature of people as human beings and a humane approach toward working with them. Subjectivity, the self and potential for growth are prized. There is a belief in the ability of people to choose, develop and change, to be responsible and control their lives. It is a positive, optimistic approach to humans as whole beings with unique perceptions and interpretations of their world. The practice of many 'caring professions' is influenced by humanistic principles via the professions' culture, identity and as guiding construct for competence (Gilfoyle, 1984). However, it is not universal. For example, medical practitioners tend to use trait theory believing in genetic determinants which are less amenable to change.

The responsibility for judging incompetence may cause a conflict between therapist and educator values and roles. The term judgement is used because it acknowledges the judicial nature of assessment where all the objective and subjective evidence is weighed. The description of 'teacher-as-judge' is apt because assessment 'differentiates children on the basis of their intellectual – and often social – skills in preparation for the social and occupational roles which the teacher perceives they will eventually play' (Hoyle, 1969, quoted in Geary, 1998, p. 242). Failure is an expected outcome, albeit for a minority. This creates the tension. 'As therapists we are not judgmental. We don't give patients pass or fails. We value them, recognise their intrinsic worth and focus upon their strengths to compensate for disabilities.' This causes discomfort when making judgements because they are integral to the role of assessor. Conflict can be most acute for those with direct responsibility for the decision making, particularly if they are inexperienced and still negotiating the transition from practitioner to educator. An experienced academic acknowledged it to be an unresolved conflict because 'sitting in judgement conflicts with a deeply held philosophy of life about unconditional positive regard'.

Breaching the boundary between therapist and educator roles is another cause of conflict. Jarvis defines education as 'any planned series of incidents, having a humanistic basis, directed towards the participants learning and understanding'. The humanistic base is 'concerned about the welfare and humanity of the participants and it is humane' (Jarvis, 1983, p. 26). This is also the basis for therapy. The commonality makes boundary transgressions easy, especially for inexperienced educators, personal tutors and those with clinical experience in psychiatry, psychotherapy or learning disabilities. The temptation 'to treat students' has been reported in social work (Ford and Jones, 1987; Howard, 1979; Towle, 1954) and occupational therapy. For example: 'I worked with adolescents in a client-centred way. I do the same as a lecturer. The values about the quality of the relationship, respect and responsibility are compatible. Sometimes I am tempted to "take on" a student as a therapist. I know this isn't appropriate and I have not got the time. I had to "harden up". I wasn't warned or informed about this when I started teaching.' If a fail scenario is viewed as a work stress then reverting to the familiar and satisfying role may be an adaptive response to anxiety. Perhaps, adopting the therapist role is a self-protective mechanism by 'doing' rather than freezing or flight. (Shipley, 1990). Another argument relates to professional socialisation: 'It is difficult not to be therapeutic. Being a therapist and teacher are similar. I take a Rogerian stance – there are gains in confidence as the student learns and becomes. Learning becomes a part of you, it is why therapists are certain beings and the training inculcates values and attitudes. Conflict is inevitable' (manager).

Although conflict may cause role strain, it is not an acceptable excuse for role blurring. There are fundamental differences in the goals and methods of education and therapy. These were described by a manager:

'in the early days as a teacher I was too therapeutic, thinking of ways to improve the student's situation. I was forgetting their responsibilities. I was providing too many safety nets and doing too much for them.' Professional obligation and a long-term perspective are the ultimate reasons for role separation: 'It is difficult, but we should positively fail some students. My convictions are stronger following visits to a department where I was embarrassed by the therapists' (work-practice organiser).

The conflict in humanistic values and roles may be caused by the stereotypes, especially the irrational association between failure on a task and as a person. 'We know that academic inadequacy robs a human of a sense of usefulness, of competency, of acceptance, of power' (Ungerleider, 1985). The causal connections between teaching and learning is another external influence can make failure difficult.

Causal theory of teaching

The causal theory of teaching (Ericson and Ellett, 1987) can exert a subtle and not so subtle influence upon staff, departments and training institutions. This epitomises a 'blame culture' which demands accountability. Student failure is attributed to poor teaching. There is assumed to be a simple cause and effect relationship with teachers accepting sole responsibility for learning outcomes, whereas learning is a complex process and partnership which is susceptible to many confounding variables. Stevens and Pihl (1987) observe 'persistent failure in schools can emanate from myriad causes. Intellectual, cultural and experiential deprivation, social and personal conflicts, behavioural deficits and learning disability... aetiology is often difficult to determine' (p. 333). Yet this myth of a causal theory of teaching is implicit and explicit in the literature, for example: 'Periodic assessment of trainees also allows educators to determine the success of their teaching' (McLeod and Harden, 1985, p. 188). Such statements tend to perpetuate an attitude of ownership, or investment by the teacher and school, to guarantee success. However, the causal theory of teaching can be countered by evidence. For example, Strauss and Sawyer (1986), using an educational production model, report a 1 per cent increase in teaching quality results in a 'modest' mean student achievement of 0.5–0.8 per cent.

This theory has a pervasive influence. It seems to contribute to assessors' sense of guilt and failure. These feelings derive from faulty attributions of responsibility for the failure and lack of differentiation between teaching and learning. This is expressed in the next quotation which also hints at the self-interrogation: 'feelings of failure as a supervisor. Did I do enough?' Confidence in supervisory abilities with other students and staff may be reduced, especially if the fail grade is seen as 'evidence of their own worth' (Eble, 1976, p. 116).

The fear of tarnishing reputations is also associated with a causal theory of teaching. This may include the reputation of staff with their colleagues, with students via 'the grapevine' and with the educational establishment. For example: 'I felt guilty, as though I had not done my job properly as a supervisor. What would the school think and say about me?' The number of fails is a mediating factor in academic settings. A few, between one and three for example, may be acceptable, but many more may raise questions about the appropriateness of the standards being applied. The meaning of the number of fails would seem to connect personal ownership and institutional performance indicators, especially whether they are perceived as a reflection of poor teaching or rigorous standards. However, the greater the number of fails, the more the balance tips towards blame. 'Student failure [in a high school] is a common, persistent and complex subject... some students will fail despite everyone's best efforts...a teacher can fail students and still be a good teacher who is doing a good job. When large numbers fail, something is wrong' (Stabile, 1989, p. 28).

The causal theory of teaching may be manifest in an institutional ethos of guaranteed success for all entrants. This ignores the fallibility of selection processes and learning as maturational process during which students may develop in all sort of ways. Nevertheless, high attrition rates, whether due to voluntary or involuntary reasons, can threaten financial viability and the reputation of a training institution. Attention has been given to early identification and assisting 'at risk' students to succeed, especially in the United States (Croen et al., 1991; Gutman et al., 1998; Lengacher and Keller, 1990; Rozier, Gilkeson and Hamilton, 1992). Although these strategies are a 'matter of institutional survival' (Gupta, 1991, p. 693) they give an impression of an investment and vested interest in ensuring all successful applicants pass. This impression is supported if the training institution disputes the judgement of the assessor especially work-based supervisors and at an appeal hearing. It can exacerbate an assessor's feeling of self-doubt and anger when a difficult decision is overturned. Supervisors are especially vulnerable to pressure to pass, often against their better judgement. It has been reported by teachers (Norcross, 1991), health visitors and general practitioners (Green, 1991), social workers (Howard, 1979), nurses (Symanski, 1991) and occupational therapists (Ilott, 1993).

Financial viability is another external pressure which connects individuals and institutions. Funding systems increasingly are linked to completion rates and involve money being taken back if students drop out. While the definition of wastage may be problematic the costs are indisputable. The Department for Education and Employment in the United Kingdom published a drop-out rate of 17 per cent for full-time and sandwich undergraduate courses in the academic year 1992–93. In 1993 the Audit Commission calculated the cost of non-completion in further and higher education as £330 million a year. A moderate drop-out rate may be viewed as a healthy sign, indicating intellectual rigour. Such substantial losses, however, create a counter-pressure. It is perhaps unsurprising that where there is a direct link between funding and output this has 'made tutors reluctant to fail students on their courses' (Scott-Clarke, 1996).

There are other institutional pressures linked to a casual theory of teaching. Contracts between education commissioners and providers tend to emphasise quantitative outputs rather than the value added gained from the educational process or longer term outcomes. Educational establishments are frequently judged by student results in league tables, the actual and symbolic dimensions of which reverberate across the whole of education. This ranges from the 'expulsion of low-grade children...[to] bounties in the form of scholarships are paid to transferring sixth formers' (Jenkins, 1996). There is increasing concern about grade inflation in higher education with the average honours classification rising from 2:2 to 2:1 in many subjects during the last 20 years. At the same time students 'whose performance is judged unsatisfactory by those teaching and assessing them' (Wright, 1996) are awarded pass and third class honours degrees.

Institutional context

The third and final element comprises facets within academic and work settings. Some are tangible and others are rituals; some facilitate while others corrupt decision making. They range from the apprenticeship model of supervision which contains the contradictory roles of collaborator and assessor, to 'pass lists' as a public denial of fails. All seem to add to the complexity of fail scenarios.

Settings: failing is more difficult in work-based settings

Most vocational training combines examination of academic ability and a period of supervised work experience. There is considerable variation within the professions about the proportion of time, weighting and importance given to these two components, especially whether practice is assessed, and if so by whom – by work-based or academic staff or a combination of both – and whether the assessment contributes towards the honours classification. However, these differences of detail do not obscure a common feature – that failing seems to be more difficult in work settings.

Failing is viewed as easier in academic settings because the whole process of assessment is 'cleaner' (lecturer). The following lists the perceived benefits for staff and student. In academic settings staff are supported by such things as:

- objective marking criteria and answer guidelines
- team rather than individual decision making
- access to the student's profile of performance for the whole course
- a system of cross marking and moderation which 'shields' individuals

There were also advantages for the student. For example, 'students can say they misread the question or didn't revise. They are always able to find excuses. This is not so when they are being assessed as a person' (work-practice organiser). Such excuses allow a shift of causal attributions from a personal reason, which is close to a student's sense of self, to a more distant cause without effecting their image or sense of control (Snyder and Higgins, 1988).

Assigning a fail grade in work settings is considered more difficult for two main reasons: the context and the assessment process. Practice settings are usually characterised by unpredictability, uncontrollable and multiple events happening simultaneously. 'The clinical setting is an unknown situation. The student may not understand, lack confidence' (supervisor). Although most realistic for assessing competence to practise the setting and supervisory relationship can interact to sabotage the process. Subjective assessment criteria, especially the 'undefinable concept of competent to practise' (lecturer) and professional unsuit-ability may result in unclear expectations and 'woolly decision making' (manager). The lack of standardisation between work-based assessors makes failing 'feel more personal and real' (work-practice organiser). The closeness of the supervisory relationship which may last for several weeks or months is another factor. Supervision comprises multiple roles including counsellor, collaborator and assessor (Boydell, 1986; Smyth, 1986; Wong and Wong, 1987). Supervisors are usually expected to nurture personal and professional development and then judge the attainment of minimum standards and beyond. The one-to-one relation-ship 'causes much more angst. The supervisor can be very exposed. They have nowhere to hide' (work-based organiser). Supervision often involves regular meetings for review, feedback and action planning. These are critical and involve 'giving the bad news', i.e. the formative and summative assessment during a personal encounter. It requires great skill to convey such feedback constructively in an honest and sensi-tive way. Strategies for coping and giving feedback are contained in Chapter 6.

Other aspects of the practice setting may add to the difficulties. The supervisor may be isolated, especially if working single-handedly. They do not have the 'authority of the HEI behind them'. They are unlikely to be familiar with the intricacies of assessment or appeals regulations. This is why a good outreach network of work-based organisers from the academic establishment is essential. Work-based organisers are external agents who oversee the assessment process. They offer support to the supervisor and student, act as independent advisers to ensure the 'right decision is made for the right reason' and provide advice and informa-tion about alternative supervisory strategies, assessment regulations, procedures and documentation.

Institutional distancing mechanisms

Assessors may feel directly responsible for awarding a fail grade, even though institutional structures such as examination boards can to some extent formalise, anonymise and diffuse the responsibility. Yet the responsibility can still be keenly felt. Some procedures would seem to be more helpful than others. Independent double and triple marking, specific assessments with 'tight answer and marking guidelines' and in other settings internal and external examiners or moderators (and students in instances of student-negotiated assessment), provide lecturers with 'reassuring confirmation and validation of your judgement'.

There is increasing formality as the process shifts from individual to group responsibility and decision making. The process usually becomes more objective and formal to comply with assessment regulations about the pass mark, options for referral, deferral and compensation. The interpretation and implementation of the regulations is often vested in an examination board. This body will normally accept collective responsibility for approving the pass list. The board may merely ratify or 'rubber stamp' the recommendations made by the manager (head of school, course leader or programme director) confirm the decisions made at the pre-board meeting between internal and external examiners, or review and adjust the marks awarded, thereby changing or 'interfering' with earlier judgements.

The assessment rules and regulations may be perceived as institutionally sanctioned mechanisms for separating the member of staff from the consequences of their judgement. For example, there is progression from lecturers' comments to numerical symbols of performance according to an agreed grading scale. Deliberation usually moves from internal through external examiners to formal course committees and examination boards. These operate regulations approved by the course, departmental, institutional and professional hierarchies. This means there is an increase in distance and anonymity between the assessor and student. The organisational ritual of posting a pass list on a notice board is an extreme example of anonymity which occurs in secondary and higher education. Those who have failed are (obviously) excluded from the 'pass' list. It is as though the institution were denying or was ashamed of their existence. Turner (1996) describes posting A level results as a 'sadistic tradition ... reminiscent of the medieval habit of displaying severed heads on pikes at the city gate'. Interestingly, these mechanisms are ineffective. They do not seem to reduce the work stress or protect staff with direct responsibility for making such judgements as staff still frequently experience the conflict between their roles and values. Academic examiners are required to contain their 'ritual power as [they] live up to a particular role expectation' (Travers, 1982, p. 285).

The range of institutional distancing mechanisms and rituals, from ratifying results through anonymous examination boards, through 'pass lists' posted on notice boards to the timing of retrieval assessments at the end of a holiday seem to be of limited value. All depersonalise the student and assessor by diffusing their responsibility in the decision-making process. They devalue, through the process of denial, the losses associated with closure of relationships with academic staff, especially those with a pastoral relationship, and with peers within the cohort.

Costs and benefits of failure

The final section in this chapter summarises the costs and benefits of a fail. Costs are incurred by individuals and institutions. The business ethic, with an internal market within the public services, has focused attention upon income and expenditure at all levels. Assigning a fail grade is costly in terms of the time, money and distress. Costs are critical for viability. However, these financial and hidden human costs need to be balanced against the long-term costs of litigation and an incompetent professional.

Time is money for all concerned

Time is money and fails require 'an inordinate amount of time' (head of school). Nevertheless there are few references to time, either for ordinary or problematical students in the literature. For example, Davenhall (1985) notes 20 minutes for report-giving meetings and Yerxa (1986) describes a range of 1.5 to 4 hours for those who display 'particularly difficult problems'. The time varies with the roles and responsibilities of those concerned. These are outlined below for examiners, work-practice organisers and managers in order to illustrate the nature of this issue.

Managers

Managers, whether called course leaders, programme directors or heads of school, are usually accountable for the action and responsible for informing the student of the result. They may undertake a range of tasks which include confirming the fairness and objectivity of the decision-making process; organising procedural arrangements, particularly the documentation in preparation for an appeal; liaison with external bodies; helping staff; and supporting the student. In total 'it takes a lot of time, in the sense of time and psychologically. All the time thinking through all the issues.' Work-practice organisers, the academic staff responsible for coordinating all work placements, also play an indirect part. This can involve more visits, incurring extra travel expenses to the work place to meet with the student and supervisor; discussion with academic colleagues to obtain a profile of the student's performance; arranging a retake placement, preparing the supervisor and student for the retake placement; following-up and supporting the supervisor; maintaining telephone contact; and record keeping. The next quotation summarises their more distant, organisational concerns: 'I hope that in the end the supervisor feels supported and has made the right decision. The student is reasonably whole for coping with the next placement. The supervisor at the retake placement feels comfortable and has the necessary information because this takes extra responsibility.'

Academic assessors

Those with direct responsibility for judging competence are likely to continue to have the most practical and emotional involvement with the student. Lecturers report using the time for many tasks. These include:

- marking, remarking, double and triple marking
- discussions about scripts and performance
- providing extra tutorials and detailed feedback on extra practice assignments to setting resit papers
- discussion with colleagues including the work-practice organiser and personal tutor and other 'interminable meetings'
- counselling and supporting the student through their anger and disappointment.

Again, it was described as 'enormously difficult, very time consuming at a practical, thinking and emotional level'. One calculated 25 hours over a fortnight. The time and intensity is likely to be matched in work-based settings.

Work-based assessors

A fail usually involves supervisors in extra activities which detract from their primary work role. These comprise:

- daily and weekly feedback sessions
- more supervision and support via explaining, instructing, directing, questioning and checking the student's understanding and performance
- support for selves gained from peers both in and out of work, and from their head of department or supervisor
- contacting the school and fieldwork organisers
- 'the time, pain and sweat' involved in writing the weekly and final report.

The constraints of time and the dual demands of supervision and service provider are acknowledged as a problem in usual circumstances but these are exacerbated with difficult students (Alsop, 1991; Green, 1991; Ilott, 1988). The work still has to be done, often in the evening which is 'very tiring'.

Financial costs

The monetary aspect links personal and institutional costs of failure. The most serious is when attrition jeopardises the financial viability of the whole programme. This was noted by a manager: 'we are poorer because the fees are gone. The cost margins on these courses are very tight anyway. But you can't think of this. It has to be separate from failing the student. I think about it afterwards and what effect it will have upon the next year. We couldn't afford to lose too many'. The effect, particularly of loss in the first year is an empty place for the rest of the course which 'is the equivalent of a third of a staff salary'. This highlights the conflict between accounts and personal costs, professional standards and financial viability for 'it is kinder for students to fail earlier rather than later in the course'. The other cost is the wastage of a training place which may be precious due to the shortfall of practitioners.

Other costs, direct and indirect, may also extend over time. These include the reputation of the programme with education commissioners: 'with more regional health authorities sponsoring students, the losses/failures will be viewed politically. This is going to be a minefield'. The costs of a student appeal against the decision are considerable. In 1991 one manager costed her time at £1,000. In 1996 a seven-year appeal procedure had cost the educational institution £70,000. These examples from one profession are mirrored for the 'explosion in legal work involving schools, colleges and universities [which] is creating fertile territory for lawyers' (Slapper, 1996). Dissatisfied students are increasingly suing educational institutions for breach of contract and negligence. One aspect of this is the upsurge in appeals against assessment judgements whether at GCSE or PhD level. Such cases are costly for all concerned, involving time, money, bad publicity and distress. These problems may be exacerbated by complaints procedures which are 'slow, anachronistic, secretive or apparently cosy' (THES, 1996). Appeals highlight the need for good assessment practice to ensure and prove 'duty of care'. These are considered in Chapters 5 and 6.

Personal costs for individuals and groups

The degree of emotional distress makes assigning a fail grade a work stress. 'It costs in personal energy. It is so mentally exhausting' (lecturer). The decision making may involve self-interrogation, deliberation and 'heart searching'. Even though the outcome is within an assessor's control it can still provoke guilt and 'a sense of failure when you have put in a lot of effort to stop them failing'.

It is also important to acknowledge the distressing nature of failure for the student, particularly if it is a new experience. The costs noted by staff included extension to the length of the course with loss of income, a waste of their time and money. Also, loss of self-esteem, feelings of guilt, dismay, disappointment and grief. They suggested two mediating variables. First, the degree of insight and expectation gained through self-evaluation and self-assessment. Second, the stage of training, the later in the course being considered most damaging and wasteful.

Personal costs may also be dispersed within the staff and student group. For example, in academic settings 'staff can go on too much. It is a new area for them' (manager), even though failing is part of their role as teacher-as-judge. There may be fear amongst the cohort 'their year is being peeled away. Who will be next?' There may be reverberations in the practice setting – 'the student put a taint on the whole department' with unfavourable comments from colleagues about reductions in caseload or productivity.

But there are benefits too

Although costs are difficult to quantify, failure, as well as being an expensive option, can also be seen as a benefit. It is important to appreciate the possibility of positive outcomes for the student, staff, educational establishment and profession. This relates to the purpose of assessment, which is not to protect the welfare of the student, nor the image of the teacher, but to protect the future recipients of the service (Ford and Jones, 1987). The positive outcomes challenge the stereotypes about failure. But more importantly, by understanding the long-term benefits, an examiner's stress may be alleviated and prevent the guilt of 'allowing student to just pass'.

The positive outcomes for the student, although identified by assessors do mirror other research from the students' perspective. Staff report a mixture of immediate, short-term and long-term benefits. Failing may hold a variety of meanings including:

- Extra time for consolidation of learning. The spin-offs for learning were noted by a work-practice organiser: 'It is amazing how they mature and overtake their peers who passed first time. They become more confident and competent. It is lovely when they come back and say "I needed to fail". It helped confirm my commitment to occupational therapy. In my experience, these students make better therapists and supervisors in comparison with those for whom everything is a doddle.'
- A catalyst for change to a more satisfying career. This longer term perspective is often available to academic staff who knew of ex-students 'writing for references and saying they are really happy'.
- A relief, ending a struggle to succeed or fulfil a parental career goal. A practice organiser described the physical expression of relief 'It was her resit placement. She was anxious, fearful and silent. She had been really hard work. We tried everything. The supervisors had no option but to fail her. Within 30 minutes she had changed. It was as though a

huge weight had been lifted from her shoulders. Her father thought occupational therapy would be a nice career for her. Six months later she wrote to thank us.' Contrary to expectations some students 'manipulate the circumstances so they will fail'.

These examples illustrate personal meanings and family factors which can complicate a fail scenario. Also, the importance of understanding the student's perspective, their self-evaluation and the connotative meaning which contains the broader implications of the symbol 'fail grade' with its emotional tone and social value (Pollio et al., 1989).

Staff also identified a number of positive outcomes for themselves. These derive from satisfaction of having the courage to fulfil their professional obligations. The experience of surviving gave them confidence for the future 'I know I am able to handle the pressure'. Supervisors reported reappraising their role 'we now monitor students in a more rounded way'. Acting as a reflective practitioner and survivor seemed to stimulate a sense of control and confidence. This was a positive outcome for the supervisor and future students. Experience also reinforces effective supervisory strategies.

Benefits are possible for the programme and education institution too. Credibility can be enhanced through demonstrable concern with upholding standards. This was perceived to be valuable for students, staff, supervisors and the 'outside world'. There was relief following the removal of students who were a 'destructive element...or one who has been a thorn in the flesh'. Other benefits flowed from a review of assessment regulations especially the 'removal of loopholes'. It stimulated increased effort within the cohort and staff team. There were similar positive outcomes for work-based assessors, especially 'they have learnt to differentiate between competence and incompetence, to be more critical'.

Finally, and most importantly, are the positive outcomes for the profession. We believe this long-term benefit is the most important reason for assigning a fail grade. It reflects the assessment rationale related to registration to practise to protect the public by ensuring they are treated by a competent practitioner.

All these benefits can be set against the negative stereotypes about failure. There are costs but there can also be immediate benefits even for the student. For example, 'it was as if a great burden had been lifted from her shoulders. She wanted to leave but felt she was letting people down. She had been living a lie, keeping up a front. When she failed it was a tremendous relief. She needed the decision to be made for her' (supervisor). Other positive outcomes are more long term, reinforcing the coping strategy of placing a fail within a temporal and professional perspective. The fair, accurate assessment of competence to practise is essential for the integrity of the practitioner and profession. The clients may be 'vulnerable people in an area of vital need' (Duffy, 1987, p. 13) who have implicit trust in the judgement and action of the professional. The potentially negative long-term outcomes of dangerous practice and costly litigation should outweigh the immediate trauma, which should be survivable.

Conclusion

The multifaceted model presented in this chapter is intended to help assessors understand the complex, interacting factors which help or hinder making judgements at the margins of competence. Even though each fail is unique, the model can be applied to a particular situation. It disentangles the complex set of individual, institutional and external factors which can impinge upon staff. This is important with increasing accountability for results in academic and vocational qualifications. All need to be assured of fair judgements, based upon best assessment practices, to protect the rights and responsibilities of all the stakeholders.

Chapter 4
Feelings exacerbate the difficulties

Introduction

Assigning a fail grade can be one of the most challenging responsibilities, especially where there is co-terminosity of registration to practise a profession and an academic award. It is a 'double whammy' for the student and assessor. Failing may result in termination of a course and a career goal. The assessor is required to discharge conflicting responsibilities to ensure justice to the student, to maintain the value of the qualification and to fulfil the role in the vocational certification process which is entrusted to a profession by society. This, added to the reasons presented in the previous chapter, is why making pass-fail decisions in professional training can be so difficult.

There is another equally important reason. This is the feelings of examiners during the decision-making process and when conveying the news. The affective responses of assessors as they make judgements at the boundary between competence and incompetence will be examined in this chapter. Judgement is a key concept. 'Assessment is a matter of judgement, not simply of computation' (CNAA, 1992, p. 91). Examiners' judgement is prized. It is enshrined in academic freedom and regulations which do not permit 'their academic judgement...[to] be questioned or overturned' (1992, p. 91). Decision making is informed by thinking and feelings, influenced by objectivity and subjectivity. Feelings are significant at each stage of a fail scenario. Communicating a fail result is another form of 'breaking bad news'. While this is recognised as difficult, requiring special skill and training in relation to medicine (informing of death or terminal illness) or management (informing those made redundant or disciplinary interviews) it seems to have been ignored in education.

Educational literature contains few references to examiners' feelings whether in ordinary or extraordinary circumstances. While the 'salience of feelings to competence, in teaching, as in other professional domains' was noted by Leat (1993, p. 505), most attention has been given to cognitive processes. When affective reactions are reported, it is the emotional stress of failing which is common across professions, countries and time. Nurse educators in the United States, Canada and the United Kingdom describe failing as 'one of the most emotionally taxing responsibilities...for it presents an emotional struggle...and awareness of one's own fallibility' (Meisenhelder, 1982, p. 348). It can be 'frustrating and debilitating' (Carpenito, 1983). Turkett (1987) noted the mutual distress: 'when faced with the reality of failure, both student and educator become uncomfortable, tense and depressed...[they] feel insufficient and powerless...both feel like failures' (p. 246) A fail grade can cause rancour: 'You can be made to feel like an ogre. The outcome was hardly worth the hassle. I felt like a trouble maker' (Lankshear, 1990, p. 37). It is the emotional exhaustion which can make failing a work stressful. Working with failing students and failing clinically unsafe students was rated as the second and third highest occupational stressors by Goldenberg and Waddall (1990). Examiners and institutions may experience other 'unfortunate outcomes such as burnout, loss of high calibre clinical faculty members and erosion of teaching standards' (Symanski, 1991).

Considering these consequences, it is unsurprising that failure is often avoided. Brandon and Davies (1979) summarised their 'disconcerting findings' in a study of marginal students in social work by condemning 'the reluctance of fieldwork teachers and tutors to stand firm in the defence of standards' (p. 345). This observation was mirrored by Davenhall (1985): 'outright failure, resulting in the discontinuation of nurse training, did not appear to occur at all' (p. 106). More recently, the Oxford and Cambridge Examination and Assessment Council were criticised for too generous grading of A level papers. This included failing 'only five out of 5,341 candidates' (O'Leary, 1997, p. 1).

Failing or the failure to fail are a cause of concern at all levels of education, but perhaps even more so at postgraduate level in professional training. This is because the assessor is failing a junior colleague, a fellow professional. Their licence to practise is a symbol of their initial or entry level competence. But this does not guarantee continued competence, aptitude for a specialism, success on a postgraduate course, potential for promotion or change of career direction. Green (1991) described the difficulties of failing a doctor training to be a general practitioner. The assessors lost confidence in their judgement and themselves. The bravery of the trainer was acknowledged, as was his need for support, as he 'screwed up' someone's career. The next quotation from a senior medical practitioner – a Regional Adviser for a Royal College – describes the tortuous process (with tendency to avoidance) in postgraduate, specialist medical education: 'If you care about your teaching then students become almost like your children and therefore you do not want to fail them. It is very, very difficult to come to terms with this fact and to tell the trainee that they are not suited to your specialty. You take the easy way out and pretend they will be all right with remedial teaching. So it goes on until they are years down the line and they are never going to become consultants. Someone has to tell them. Junior doctors do not fail to progress in a speciality. They demonstrate that the speciality is not the appropriate one for them. We need to tell them this early. But this takes courage and few of us have got that sort of courage.'

This is why this chapter is devoted to this seemingly hidden component of assessment. We believe it is important to understand the range of fears and feelings which may influence judgements. Some are helpful. For example, a gut feeling can act as an early warning system, sensitivity to which can direct an assessor's thinking and behaviour to obtain evidence to verify or counter their alarm. Alternatively, the fears associated with failure can result in marginal students being given the 'benefit of the doubt', allowed to 'just pass' or given extraordinary amount of support to ensure a pass grade. Such avoidance is not necessarily 'unprofessional cowardice' (Lankshear, 1990, p. 35) but may be a self-protective reaction against potentially overwhelming distress. Understanding that this stress seems to be a common, almost universal response is an important strategy for staff. Other strategies to mitigate the stress are outlined in the following sections. Acknowledging the affective dimension of assessment can inform thinking, validate feelings and strengthen assessment practices.

Failure: is difficult as a whole and at each stage

Failure is an emotionally charged word and action which can provoke a complex constellation of emotions. Many are adverse. These include guilt, anxiety, distress, personal failure and exhaustion, which have an enduring, debilitating effect, extending beyond work. This is why it is important to understand the affective aspects of assigning a fail grade. The discomfort anticipated and associated with judging incompetence may contribute to the failure to fail. Ilott's study revealed a common pattern of feelings experienced at each stage of a fail scenario. Understanding these as usual or predictable may give assessors the assurance gained from a sense of universality (Yalom, 1985). 'Other people have felt the same desolation caused by having to fail a student – not just me' (supervisor).

This book draws heavily upon the results of 30 focused interviews with academic and practice assessors who confirmed Meisenhelder's (1982) observation that 'one of the most emotionally taxing responsibilities facing an instructor today is to assign a failing clinical grade' (p. 348). The range and depth of emotions are conveyed through language, metaphor and non-verbal communication. For example, 'I felt terrible. I agonised all weekend. Was I doing the right thing? Was I being too hard? I was impossible to live with.' There was a striking commonality in descriptions. The process was 'so mentally exhausting' with decision making involving 'a lot of soul searching' and 'much heart searching'. It engendered a sense of failure and guilt. For example, 'the trauma was the worst bit. It was almost guilt because it is such a big responsibility for the profession and student' (work-based examiner) and 'we do not want students to fail – we feel failures ourselves' (lecturer). These statements reflect two main reasons why failing is difficult: the causal theory of teaching (Ericson and Ellett, 1987) and stereotypes which view failure as a 'life tragedy – the worst of all possible fates' (Meisenhelder, 1982, p. 348).

A common pattern of feelings emerged from this general background. Understanding this pattern as usual or predictable may offer assurances of universality and rationality during a 'difficult and agonising process' (lecturer). However, the value in such feelings, even when they are conflicting, was acknowledged by an experienced manager who commented, 'as me, I feel dreadful because of my relationship with the student. As a therapist I wish, I wonder why and what else we could have done to ensure success. As an educator I know it is the right thing to do, we must maintain standards. There is a real conflict between these three parts. The feelings vary with each student but I would not like to be totally detached from these feelings.' Examples of ways of coping with this pattern of feelings are included to demonstrate how the fail taboos can be confronted.

Anxiety during the decision-making phase

Anticipatory anxiety is a common feature when deciding to give a fail grade. A 'great deal of trepidation' may be combined with other feelings such as anger, distress, self-doubt, sadness and concern for the student. Academic and work settings add to the anxiety in different ways related to students knowing or not knowing the results. Examiners highlighted their stress and powerlessness while knowing – 'It is an awful time...it is a secret' – before the results are made public. In work settings a fail grade should never be a surprise. If it is, the student has been deprived of 'due process' – their right to proper supervision with regular, honest feedback. Yet, knowing is also difficult. The student may withdraw or be withdrawn by the school to avoid 'prolonging the agony...the student said she was very, very upset and could not stay till the end of the week' (work-based assessor).

The unpredictability of the students' responses and their own ability to deliver the bad news at the final report giving meeting was a major source of anxiety for work-based assessors. 'I was very conscious that anything could happen. He could respond in any way – angry, make accusations, break down.' Staff responsible for coordinating work placements also reported a degree of performance anxiety. This was related to their supportive role: 'whether I will pick up the right vibes'. There was also much self-interrogation: 'Is it me, am I nit-picking?' Assessors wondered whether with closer supervision, more time, a different practice or patient group the student could have achieved the minimum standard of competency for their stage of training.

Staff describe two main strategies for dealing with anticipatory and performance anxiety. These were confirmation of their judgement and preparation for the report-giving meeting. Verification was sought from colleagues – internal or external examiners and other members of the staff team. Managers responsible for delivering the fail grade also sought corroboration: 'I will go back over their work, reconsider and make sure that I agree with the decision and believe it is the right one.' Another described checking 'all the facts and procedures...to gain as much information both factual and intuitive. I am concerned to get everything right.' This is especially important as procedural irregularity is grounds for a student appeal.

Coping while giving a fail grade

Relief and anxiety seem to be common feelings experienced during the exit interview. The tension between relief, because of the student's knowledge of results, and anxiety due to the unpredictability of the response (both of individuals and the cohort), was illustrated by a lecturer: 'once the results are posted – this is built up as a big thing – it doesn't seem so bad. You can alleviate the tension on a face-to-face basis. The next teaching slot is not liked by tutors. You go into the office, shut the door and put the "do not disturb" notice up.'

During the final meeting staff report concentrating upon managing the interaction and assisting the student to plan for the future. Listening, attending or counselling skills are used to focus upon the student's needs, feelings and to prevent feeling a failure. The interaction is likely to be determined by the student's reaction. It could be 'easy if they are realistic, relieved. Then they are kind to you. If it is a surprise then I am supportive. If they are angry then I feel angry and defensive' (manager). The student's response elicited conflicting emotions, often experienced simultaneously. For example, 'very apprehensive and also sorry for her'. Achieving a balance between positive and negative was summarised as 'I wish it was not happening, but also want to make it as positive as possible'. It is perhaps unsurprising that such emotional turbulence causes exhaustion and desire to avoid similar situations, and also why inexperienced assessors are vulnerable, especially if they do not expect to be 'bullied...I meant my comments to be helpful and was hurt when she said they were derogatory...I now ask students what they mean and whether they are only seeking praise. It was a hard lesson but one that I have never forgotten.' The term 'bullying' may be incongruous with the image of vocational training, yet it recurs, especially in work settings and the literature. Displaced anger (Meisenhelder, 1982), resentment and annoyance (Wilson, 1972), open rejection (Lawrence, 1985) and controlled rage (Ungerleider, 1985) have all been reported. Such responses require understanding and assertiveness. Anger is a natural response to disappointment and bad news. Assessors may need to be assertive, providing evidence from detailed examples to explain and counter any attempts at coercion to change the result.

Other strategies include the use of colleagues as a source of confirmation and support during the final meeting. This was especially so in academic settings: 'there are always two people, the course leader and the personal tutor.' In work settings this supportive role may be undertaken by the work-practice organiser acting 'as an arbitrator, making sure everyone has really heard what has been said'. A remedial approach can be appropriate for a first fail. This involves identifying the problem and ways of rectifying it. Whether it was a first or final fail, examiners will usually wish to manage the enquiring/report-giving interview in a non-judgmental, clear way which ensures the dignity of all parties.

A humane system of notification which allows a proper closure of relationships is important for dealing with a student's distress. Managers responsible for informing the student described using strategies which acknowledged the student's present distress and also their potential by placing the fail within a longer, life-span perspective. This approach was used to 'guide from negative to a positive, to a programme of action and what they have learnt during their period of training and the failure'. This contrasts with the anonymous, impersonal ritual of posting results on a public notice board which still does not seem to reduce the trauma for the examiner.

'I have a system. They receive their results in an envelope to take away and open. It contains a note saying they have failed, they must be very upset and when they feel ready, I will be waiting to see them. I wait five minutes, or a day, or they do not appear at all. It finishes me off if they go and we never hear from them again. At the start I say they must be feeling very angry and this is all right. This usually leads to tears or fury. I allow this, this isn't the moment to discuss what went wrong, they need time to settle into what is happening. I ask them to write notes about what they want to talk about and do, so they can come back the next day to discuss these. Most do come back, then we talk about the future. It is now the worst thing and they don't think any thing good can come from it, but they are also relieved. I offer three options: referral to the careers service, the procedure for appeal if they still wish to be an occupational therapist, or providing a reference to help their future plans. We also discuss how they will tell other people. I write to them two weeks later asking if there is anything I can do to help. About 50 per cent reply. A fail is bad news. Anger is a healthy response. I feel better and so does the student.'

Such a system is sensitive to the feelings and needs of both parties. It recognises the need for closure to minimise the distress of 'unfinished business'.

Feelings which linger after the student has gone

Those with direct responsibility for judging incompetence felt relief when the student left. Relief was mixed with other emotions. For example, 'guilt and relief that it was all over, she was leaving the department and we didn't have to struggle any more'. Regret and guilt were due to several factors. These included self-doubt, self-interrogation, a sense of personal failure for not achieving a successful outcome: 'we had failed to get him through.' Inexperienced examiners were susceptible to identification with the student: 'I kept putting myself in her shoes, thinking about how I might have felt. Her father collected her, mine would have done the same.' This illustrates the hazards of the loss of emotional distance when the examiner experiences affective empathy (Maslach, 1982). There were fears for their or the department's reputation for being the 'ogre who failed students'.

Distress can be contagious, spreading within a department and to other students. Departure means an end, which allows return to a normal routine: 'We could get back to work, to normality and peace of working with patients rather than spending all the time with the student.' Work-based staff may loose confidence in their supervisory abilities: 'I did not dare to have the next student.' They described requiring a break to rest and recuperate. This lasted months to a year before they were willing, or wanted to be asked to supervise another student. They were apprehensive: 'We were very careful and wary with the next one. We were frightened of doing the wrong thing.' These illustrate the enduring impact of fail scenarios.

Finally, staff reported pride for fulfilling their professional obligation in protecting threshold standards. The reassurance for making the right decision for the right reason was acknowledged: 'We never had any doubts afterwards.' Fails provide a learning opportunity for even the most experienced academic staff: 'I learn from every one about what to do and what to avoid. It is emotionally draining and I need a lot of support' (manager).

Causal attributions can explain some examiners' affective responses

Attribution theory provides a useful conceptual framework for understanding an examiners' affective responses, especially when judgements are made about effort, ability and difficulty of the task. The interplay between effort and ability, as two causes of success or failure in achievement-related situations, influences assessors. Effort is an internal, unstable and controllable factor (Tollefson and Chen, 1988). Staff seem to define effort as interest, enthusiasm, commitment, motivation and attendance. In attributional terms, ability is an internal, stable and uncontrollable factor. An assessor's feedback and affective response may be influenced by attributions of effort and ability. This can be expressed in the desire to reward effort, to allow hard work to compensate for deficits in ability. Students whose 'ambitions are beyond their abilities' evoke protectiveness, sympathy and distress. Alternatively, there is a tendency to penalise able students who succeed by 'skimming the surface', expending minimal effort. Examiners can feel sympathy when effort exceeds ability and anger when ability is not matched by effort (Graham, 1984). The impact of this disequilibrium between effort and ability was noted by a work-based examiner: 'If they are working hard but still failing, there is a temptation to pay them for their effort by giving them the benefit of the doubt. It is easy and you want to do this...If they are lazy and not bothering, then a fail grade gives them a kick up the backside.' The primacy of effort was reiterated by an experienced manager: 'They would be marked up or down. You would not be human if you didn't. If the student seeks and appreciates the help given, it is bound to influence you. Whereas, if they do not attend or show any effort ...'

Inappropriate attribution of responsibility may engender intense, enduring feelings of guilt. Lack of effort and disinterest are key reasons for assigning a fail grade. They seem to make staff angry, irritated and embarrassed. Effort attributions elicit stronger affective reactions than ability attributions (Raviv et al., 1983). This illustrates the links between cognitions, affective responses and action, especially 'that thoughts determine feelings' (Graham, 1984, p. 91) and that 'affect plays an essential role, serving as the key link between thought (i.e. the attribution) and action' (Prawat, Byers and Anderson, 1983, p. 138).

The kaleidoscope of feelings can differ according to a variety of factors. Irritation, exasperation and anger reflect 'an "ought" emotion that often accompanies the belief that the target of anger is capable of changing behaviour' (Graham, 1984, p. 93). The relationship with the student seems to be important. It is rewarding to work with an interested student, to nurture development and progression, whereas frustration is provoked by lack of effort. This reflects the complexity of attributional dimensions and how 'a composite measure of teachers' sympathy, grading and willingness to help students decreased as the attribution for failure went from ability to strategy to effort' (Clifford, 1986a, p. 82). The stage of training is another factor which appears to influence strategy and attributions of responsibility: 'I am more supportive with a first-year student, giving directions on how to improve because I want to facilitate change and success. With a finalist student I have to deal with my feelings of failure and their failure. It involves re-building with different strategies and not answering the question for them.' This is important. Priority needs to be given to achieving threshold standards rather than rewarding or punishing too much or too little effort, for the credibility of the profession.

Failure to fail: passing to avoid failing

Reasons for passing a failing student

This and the previous chapter would seem to confirm failing as one of the most stressful duties of an assessor. Unsurprisingly, it is often avoided.

This occurs when a pass grade is awarded to those who have not yet reached and, more worryingly, may never attain the minimum standard required for safe, effective practice. Marginal students are given the 'benefit of the doubt' or allowed to 'just pass'. This has been reported in a range of professions. Nearly 25 per cent of 475 staff attending 23 workshops held between 1988-97 admitted in a public forum they had avoided failing. 'I recently made a decision on a borderline student. I now regret passing them. It was my lack of confidence.' This is an alarmingly high incidence of the 'failure to fail' (Lankshear, 1990, p. 35). This figure is supplemented by anecdotal evidence. For example, supervisors award a pass, but then write a separate letter expressing concern that the student had been accepted for training. Similarly they may refuse to employ a student who had just successfully completed a final placement with them. A similar strategy has been noted in medicine where a junior doctor receives a 'splendid reference' to ensure the trainee gets a post in another region. It is easy to condemn such examples as a gross abdication of professional responsibility. This book is intended to help examiners transfer the bravery implicit in such disclosure into the courage required to assign a fail grade. This involves understanding why examiners avoid a fail grade.

During the focused interviews occupational therapy assessors with direct responsibility recalled a student they should have failed almost as vividly as those they had failed. They gave five main reasons for avoidance:

- the conflict in values between therapist and educator
- lack of evidence especially about inappropriate attitudes
- difference between professional suitability and academic ability
- inexperience
- and finally, just to avoid failure.

These reasons mirror those presented in Chapter 3 as to why failing students is difficult.

Conflict in values

The conflict in roles between educator and therapist was the most frequently cited reason for passing a failing student. The multifaceted reasons are illustrated by a supervisor: 'Partly being a therapist. If the student is well motivated am I just another hurdle in their way? Partly to avoid the hassle. Perhaps I don't know. Am I able to make the judgement?' Other confounding variables include the difficulty discriminating between ability and effort, especially the desire to reward effort, some but not sufficient improvement. This reflects the humanistic value of working from and emphasising strengths: 'She had worked very, very hard. She was better but still not up to scratch for her stage of training. We didn't want to

"knock her back" because she had tried and appreciated our feedback.'
Teachers also want to reward effort. They 'were proudest and most satisfied when students, especially low ability students, succeeded through
effort' (Prawat et al., 1983, p. 142). The conflict of values was mentioned
most frequently by the most experienced managers as heads of schools:
'Giving the benefit of the doubt especially in the first year. Thinking they
will change. But early problems are often an indicator. Individually and
collectively we are too generous.'

Lack of evidence

The second major reason given for not assigning a fail grade was lack of
evidence. There may be difficulty obtaining sufficient, appropriate
evidence regarding professional unsuitability or academic weakness to
withstand the rigours of an appeal. Again, this reason consisted of several
parts. These included a subjective suspicion which was unsupported by
hard 'objective' evidence. Another was inadequate documentation, i.e. a
contemporaneous record which contained the problems in the academic
or work setting in a systematic, detailed way. There are also students who
consistently achieve 'a bare pass, those who just scrape through'. These
examples contradict commonly held assumptions about the power of
academic staff to terminate training.

Such students cause concern but academic staff can feel powerless
within the system. A manager expressed the frustration: 'there are odd
students who qualify even though I think they should not but there is
nothing in the system to prevent them from doing so. It is usually to do
with attitude and motivation but there has been nothing to "get them on".'
The assessment of affective, attitudinal and attributional qualities is notoriously problematic. However, even the American legal system expects
academic staff to exercise such judgements. For, 'by virtue of their
training, faculty members are uniquely qualified to observe and judge all
aspects of their student's academic performance...in cognitive and non-
cognitive areas' (Goclowski, 1985, p. 104). It is likely that this factor is
compounded by uncertainty about the exact nature of minimum competency to practise. In most professions this has never been defined very
precisely. This can greatly increase an assessor's uncertainty when making
borderline decisions, and if there is uncertainty about what is being
looked for to confirm minimum competence then it is even more likely
that the evidence available may be seen as inadequate to make clear
decisions (Fraser et al., 1997).

Professional suitability versus academic ability

The third reason encapsulates the increasing emphasis upon higher qualifications for status in practical, caring, vocational professions. However,

these are not and should not be incompatible because both professional suitability and academic ability are required. A lecturer described this tension: 'There was a belief that the student would make a good occupational therapist because of their personality. This was seen as separate from their academic performance. But this was unfair to the student and the profession because both are equally important.'

Inexperience

The lack of experience of fail scenarios, especially amongst supervisors, was another reason for avoidance. Academic staff reported feeling more 'able, confident to fail because of our experience whereas supervisors tend to "pass the buck"'. This confidence was not shared by new lecturers, especially if they disagreed with the outcome of collective decision making. 'I was a new teacher, insecure and lacking confidence in my decision so I did not fight for what I believed in. Within three months I was setting finalist papers. This is an awesome responsibility and no one tells you how to do it. It is not discussed. Marking is frightening.' Training courses and mentorship schemes are important to assist new staff make the transition from practitioner to educator, to understand assessment principles and gain confidence. The National Committee of Inquiry into Higher Education (1997) in the United Kingdom highlighted another benefit. It recommended, that to 'achieve world class higher education teaching, it should become the norm for all permanent staff with teaching responsibilities to be trained on accredited programmes' (p. VIII paragraph 70).

The low incidence of failure in work settings, the number of students and length of time as a supervisor all limit the opportunities to gain experience. This makes specific preparation even more necessary so assessors are able to confront the taboos, to give permission to award a fail grade and provide vicarious experience from sharing experiences (Ilott, 1995).

Avoidance of failure

The final reason was 'ducking the issue'. Avoidance may take a variety of forms. For example, from 'going off on health grounds rather than fail the student' while academic and work-based supervisors admitted to 'passing the buck'. This included 'finding reasons to push them through. For example, they've been ill, or blaming yourself for not giving them enough time.' An inordinate amount of help, 'plenty of immediate feedback, extra written work, delaying the mid-way report until the student improved' could be given to ensure a pass grade.

Avoidance may be regretted with hindsight. Academic staff observed how students can 'suffer when they fail in the second year, after I have pushed them through the first'. This contradicts the superficial and immediate benefits of 'pulling a student through'. Work-based organisers reported feeling frustrated when 'supervisors have pulled back from making the final decision. I am very cross. I do not believe a student can redeem themselves in the last week. They have been pressurised, bullied or given in to emotional blackmail.' Avoidance can also deprive students of extra learning time to consolidate and confirm their competence.

Comparing failing and not failing

Although avoidance is the easier, immediate option it seems to engender more guilt and shame in the longer term. This is due to several factors, many of which repeat reasons why failing is so difficult. These include a preference for making decisions earlier rather than later in a programme; the problems of discriminating between learning and assessment time; being seen to set threshold standards to preserve reputations, and the subjectivity of small cohorts or a one-to-one supervisory relationship. The reasons do not lessen guilt and shame from failing to fulfil their professional obligation. This reinforces the most important positive outcome. 'It felt 100 per cent right to fail the student. It would have felt worse if we had passed her. Failing the first student is the hardest. I will know next time that I can survive it. I'll have the courage not to let a poor student slip through the net.'

Assigning a fail grade requires courage and conviction. Pride is possible from making the right decision for the right reasons and satisfaction from managing the fail well. Support and debriefing can help whether failure is confronted or avoided. This can be provided by peer or external colleagues such as work-based organisers. Their role, clarifying the situation is important: 'I will ask if they are happy to work with the student if they qualified next week. If their answer is no, then I ask them to do some deep soul searching.' There is an equivalent role if failure has been avoided. This encompasses honest feedback so the student knows improvement is necessary. Also, non-judgmental follow-up with the examiner to discuss the adequacy of support offered and 'whether with hindsight they would make the same decision'.

The feelings of those indirectly involved

Assessors are not the only ones who experience a complex constellation of feelings. Those indirectly involved – including the staff group, the cohort, the student, their parents or partners and patients – would also seem to be vulnerable to the spread of stress.

The whole staff group may be affected for a variety of reasons. For example, the time requirements, the contradiction between pastoral and academic roles and the blurring of the boundary between therapy and education with the 'temptation to treat students'. Institutional rituals to distance an individual assessor from the outcome or deny the losses associated with attrition do not seem to alleviate the stress. In practice settings a marginal student 'depressed the atmosphere, the support workers were upset'. They may be a source of tension within the interprofessional team, with threats to reputations and productivity if workload is reduced.

A failure can exacerbate the fear of failure amongst the whole cohort. They may respond in a variety of ways, for example: fear – 'their year was "being peeled away" and who would be next?'; anger – 'we walked round in pairs for moral support'; acceptance – 'sometimes they just accept and don't seem to notice'; sadness – 'we underestimate the hole that is left and the effect, for example, they put out an extra seat'. The cohort may also recognise the positive outcome: 'I think the students would have been more distressed if this student had passed. He was so weak it would have jeopardised the reputation of the course.'

Fail grades can affect parents and partners too. School leavers may be fulfilling a parental career goal. If so, failure may disappoint parental expectations and there may be disapproval. Kim and Clifford (1988), in their theory of constructive failure postulate that 'self-initiated goals produce more constructive responses to failure than imposed goals' (p. 29). There may be angry, blaming reactions from fathers and spouses too as they challenge the fairness and appropriateness of the fail grade. Pollio et al. (1991) suggest parental reactions to grades be viewed as an emotional response, expressing their needs and values.

Service users also interact with and react to marginal students. The constraints of time and dual demands of supervisory and practitioner roles pervade the literature. This dilemma is brought into sharp focus if the supervisor judges the student to be untrustworthy, unsafe or dangerous (Rittman and Osburn, 1995). Liability for errors rests with the supervisor. Service users may make negative comments about the student: 'She was hesitant, quiet and was only an observer in the group. They teased her, they had her sussed out – that she didn't know how to cope with people'; 'After the student left, a number said they hadn't felt confident with the student.' Patient assessments are considered to be of limited value due to their 'failure to discriminate ... [except at] the extremes' (Henkin et al., 1990).

Conclusion

The feelings which accompany making judgements at the margins of competence may influence the quality of decision making. Fail scenarios are stressful. Feelings are an important part of the assessment process. Understanding the reasons why failing is difficult may enable assessors to confront and challenge negative stereotypes. This is necessary to reduce the incidence of avoidance or 'failure to fail'.

A complex set of contradictory emotions may be experienced during a fail scenario. Anxiety, guilt, distress and self-doubt is prevalent amongst academic and work-based assessors with direct responsibility for decision making. There seems to be a common pattern from anticipatory anxiety with anger, distress, sadness and concern; through relief and anxiety when conveying the 'bad news'; to relief, guilt, reassurance and pride for maintaining threshold standards. The unknown and unexpected facets seem to provoke the most distress. The feelings can endure and also spread to others involved at the periphery, such as the whole staff group and cohort, parents and partners and service users.

Attribution theory provides a useful theoretical framework for disentangling the impact of effort and ability. It is important to understand the interplay between effort, ability and strategy, especially how they may engender an assessor's feelings of anger or sympathy. The desire to reward effort needs to be countered. The achievement of threshold standards should be the criteria for awarding a pass grade.

There appears to be a close relationship between the reasons why failure is difficult and why fail grades are avoided. The causes include the conflict in values between education and therapy, an examiner's inexperience and identification with the student, and the problems of defining and assessing competence, especially professional suitability. We believe understanding the affective aspects is as important as the more usual cognitive and psychometric dimensions of assessment.

Chapter 5
Principles of assessment: a reminder

Introduction

This book is about the success and failure of students undertaking professional education. In the broadest sense it relates to the overall quality of professional education in preparing individuals to become entry level practitioners. Our central argument is that however good the programme, there must be an open, fair assessment system to ensure that those who fail to cross the threshold of minimum competence receive a fail grade. This requirement warrants dependable, robust assessment procedures throughout the course. Such processes span strategic levels with appeals mechanisms in higher education institutions respecting the primacy of public protection through to the detail of effective student feedback to ensure 'due process'.

Assessment at its worst can be artificial, disconnected from student learning and course objectives, and fulfilling some bureaucratic requirement to produce marks, grades or other kind of assessment outcomes, whereas effective assessments are designed to produce high quality evidence about the progress individual students are making in relation to the course aims and learning outcomes. At their best such assessments can reinforce learning rather than undermine it.

Judging evidence from assessments

All assessments involve complex decision making as 'assessors...weigh evidence which will enable them to judge "on the balance of probabilities" or "beyond reasonable doubt"' (Gonczi, 1994, p. 33). The legal metaphor is mirrored in Hoyle's phrase 'teacher-as-judge' (1969). Assessors, when weighing all the evidence of competence and incompetence, must compare the benefits and risks so as to reach a defensible conclusion which is responsible, reasonable and respectable, whereas 'beyond reasonable doubt' demands a greater burden of proof. The assessor will be expected to demonstrate substantive concern and certainty that the student should be awarded a fail grade.

Judgements are based upon a range of evidence. While the host of assessment methods used in professional education provide many types of evidence on which to judge competence and conduct, one of the most valuable is extended periods of observation in practice situations. Work placements are such a vital component of most assessment schemes that the time requirements are mandated by the professional and statutory bodies (see glossary). Such observations provide valid evidence for they provide the opportunity to assess the whole in context – working with service users in real life and coping with different professional challenges. However, the uncertainty of work settings, the dynamics of the staff–student relationship and the incidental, ephemeral nature of much of the evidence means such assessments are often considered too subjective. This is why it is important to use second opinions, so the evidence is seen and judged by several assessors, including supervisors and lecturers.

However, making judgements and being judgmental can be problematic for 'caring professions' which espouse humanistic psychology as a value base for practice. A supervisor summarised the dilemma: 'I hate making judgements about people. Who is to say that I am better or right to do so?' Although the status of teacher or supervisor confers this responsibility it does not address the underlying conflict in values. Many academic and work-based staff are expected to be teacher, assessor and personal tutor/counsellor, even though there are inherent contradictions between these roles. Employing good assessment principles is an important way of coping with any resultant role strain.

This chapter presents key elements of a good assessment system and defines some common terms such as 'validity' and 'reliability'. The importance of obtaining sufficient evidence (of both competence and incompetence) is highlighted. These principles fit within the cycle of eliciting, interpreting and acting upon the evidence derived from formative and summative assessments (Wiliam and Black, 1996). They also match the legal metaphor for they comprise obtaining, verifying and corroborating the evidence so judgements may be made either 'on the balance of probabilities' or 'beyond reasonable doubt'. However, all these need to fit within a framework of a coherent assessment schedule, training for assessors, explicit assessment criteria and effective mechanisms for student feedback.

Assessment: different types for different purposes

Assessments are usually categorised as norm or criterion referenced. Norm-referenced assessment is competitive and involves making judgements about an individual's achievement by comparing their performance with others on the same assessment. Students are placed in rank order with results plotted on a distribution curve, even in higher education where students are an elite, rather than a representative 'normal' sample of the population. In contrast, criterion-referenced assessments comprise judgements about performance against set, pre-specified criteria and standards. The focus is upon mastery with the achievement of a criter-ion representing a minimum, optimum or essential standard. National Vocational Qualifications use criterion-referenced assessments. The student is either competent or not yet competent when judged against standards set by the occupational sector.

Ideally, there should be a 'goodness of fit' between assessment method/s, learning outcomes and the purpose of assessment. There is a plethora of assessment methods – from unseen, multiple-choice examina-tion papers to group projects. A cause of concern occurs when the learning outcomes for a unit, academic level or course are over or under-assessed. This may be due to the purpose or purposes of assessment. Atkins, Beattie and Dockrell (1993) identified 13 purposes for assessment in higher education. These are:

- to establish the level of achievement reached at the end of the course or unit
- to establish progress during a course or unit and give feedback on it
- to diagnose strengths and weaknesses leading to remedial action or to extension learning
- to consolidate work done so far – a learning experience in itself
- to motivate students
- to predict a student's likely performance level in the future
- to determine whether a student is 'safe to practise'
- to select for entry to further training, employment, etc.
- to conform to the requirements of external regulatory bodies
- to give individual staff feedback on the effectiveness of their teaching
- to determine the extent to which course aims have been achieved
- to obtain information on the effectiveness of the learning environment
- to monitor standards over time. (pp. 6–7)

This list covers assessment as extrinsic motivation, results as evidence of attainment, and aptitude (or potential) as a quality assurance criteria for internal and external consumption. The reason 'to determine whether a student is "safe to practise"' introduces an extra difficulty because assess-ment of competence encompasses the triad of fitness to practise, for purpose and award as outlined in Chapter 2. The challenge is to devise valid, integrated assessments of 'competence to practise' which are reliable, practicable, economical and acceptable. Sufficient evidence must be obtained from a range of sources. The evidence is then evaluated on the 'balance of probabilities' or 'beyond reasonable doubt'. However, a note of caution. These terms represent ideals and are not an empirical truth because 'principles apply in a context. The particular context imposes constraints' (Bligh, Jaques and Warren-Piper, 1981, p. 26)). The need to choose between conflicting principles is a common constraint. Judgement at the curriculum planning stage – when the whole assessment schedule is designed – is as critical as when considering an individual student. Planning needs to be informed by research about the effectiveness of the different methods.

Principles

Validity

Validity may be considered a fundamental assessment principle but it is also one of the most difficult to apply. Validity can be thought of as representing the degree to which the method assesses what it claims or intends to assess. Although this sounds simple, Chapter 2 highlighted the difficulty of defining competence. Validity in this context is dependent upon an appropriate, acceptable and agreed definition of competence. Yet this is elusive. This paradox is apparent along the whole continuum of undergraduate, postgraduate and continued education for many professions. For example, in 1996 the Chief Medical Officer wrote 'the exact definition of competence requires further work but it is at the heart of ensuring that practising doctors in all specialities have the appropriate skills and attributes' (Calman, 1996).

Valid assessments integrate cognitive, psychomotor and affective domains in a way which is sensitive to context-specific, case-specific learning (Newble et al., 1994). This is epitomised by the integrated approach to competence which combines task and attributional models (Gonczi, 1994). It was a feature of the global definitions of 'competence to practise' and the 'unspoken consensus' about the criteria for failing discussed in chapter two. This focus upon integration – the whole in context – is the antithesis of 'the notorious "tick-box" approach' of National Vocational Qualifications. Detailed specifications have led to a mechanistic and atomistic approach to learning and assessment. Thus, 'what is integrated in reality is often disaggregated in assessment practice' (Wolf and Silver, 1995, p. 2).

Validity is not an either/or principle. It refers to the results of assessments and these are not valid or invalid. It is a matter of degree (Bligh, 1994). The different types of validity include:

- content validity: the assessment matches the content of the work
- predictive validity: the results predict future performance
- concurrent validity: the results correlate with some other measure of current, work performance
- construct validity: the assessment is constructed on the basis of a validated theory or theoretical construct
- face validity: there is strong impressionistic evidence that the assessment assesses what it is intended to assess

- ecological validity: the assessment is close to the real life situations encountered, it is authentic rather than artificial.

Using clear criteria when collecting assessment evidence

Explicit criteria enhance both the validity and reliability of the assessment process. Although the specification of criteria for judging professional practice is complex, it is an essential starting point. Clear, usable assessment criteria allow individual assessments to be compared, combined and related to explicit outcome standards for success and failure. They contribute to the openness and accountability of the whole process. Explicit criteria also counter criticisms of subjectivity, especially blaming failure upon a personality clash rather than non-attainment of baseline standards. While attempts to define competence and threshold standards are often greeted with scepticism (for example, Sutherland (1998) criticises the Quality Assurance Agency's 'search for the holy grail of single, meaningful, system-wide "threshold standards" [because it] can end only in an over-generalised description, a worthless lowest common denominator'), it is no longer acceptable to assume that experienced professionals carry around in their heads clearly defined criteria which are so obvious and universal that they do not need to be written down.

As this book is primarily about initial training and entry level competence the emphasis has been upon baseline, threshold or minimum standards to help assessors make pass–fail decisions. However, this is only the beginning of career-long learning and continued professional development. This means students need to understand and begin to work to achieve the more advanced standing which is seen to exemplify expert rather than novice standing in their chosen profession.

Reliability

Consistency is the essence of reliability. Assessments are usually expected to produce comparable outcomes, consistent standards over time, and between different students and examiners. Those which do not threaten the standard of a qualification. In 1996 the Chief Inspector of Schools criticised teachers' judgements of General National Vocational Qualifications as being 'unreliable in a quarter of schools'. The monitoring mechanism also failed in that the inconsistencies were not identified by the awarding bodies (Charter, 1996). Grade inflation, the lack of comparability between subjects and degree awarding institutions have provoked much concern about standards in the United Kingdom.

There are five types of reliability. These are:

- examiner reliability: the extent to which an examiner applies the same standard when judging different students on the same assessment

- test–retest reliability: the extent to which the same students are judged consistently on the same assessment administered on different occasions
- inter-examiner reliability: the extent to which there is consistency between different examiners, and they maintain similar, comparable standards when judging different students on the same assessment
- inter-item reliability: the extent to which students produce a consistent pattern of results or performance on different assessments, each of which is designed to test the same ability
- test reliability: the extent to which the assessment either as a whole or the component parts, produces a consistent pattern of results which are not influenced by other, irrelevant factors.

Work-based assessments are bedevilled by reliability problems. Work settings are the most authentic for judging the ability to integrate the art, science and ethics of a profession. Evidence is collected naturally in the normal context. This provides a direct link between evidence and inferences of competence. However, realism – the reality of work – is diverse. It is usually characterised by uncertainty and inconsistency of people and context. This necessitates a trade-off between reliability and validity. Also, much evidence arises spontaneously, and is incidental and ephemeral, which makes recording (and verification) even more difficult.

Meta-analyses of work-based learning affirm the difficulty of applying assessment principles in practice. The problems were summarised by Barker (1990) in the following statement: 'The criterion and factors underlying concepts and practices of clinical competence and evaluation are poorly researched and understood. Objective, comprehensive and standardised assessment measures...have not been developed and rigorously applied...many are ad hoc and neglect the planning and feedback function of supervision...[and] have limited predictive validity and are not a reliable gauge of student performance' (p. 198). Research into academic assessments suggests they are equally flawed (Atkins et al., 1993) as they share similar problems. These are outlined in the next section.

Balancing objectivity and subjectivity

So called 'objective' assessments tend to be prized. This is because they are perceived to be fair and free from bias. Objectivity represents a scientific-behaviourist approach. However, it is doubtful whether any assessment – even computer-marked assignments – are truly objective as they are devised by humans. The preceding description of validity and reliability highlights the complexity. Assessments usually involve a complex series of subjective decisions and interpretations. The outcome is a symbol – a grade, a percentage or degree classification – of this process. Bligh notes how 'frequently degree classes and grades are revered as having some mystical objectivity' (Bligh et al., 1981). Also, objectivity may be unattainable and undesirable for people working in the human services. All depend upon a cooperative relationship between the professional and the service user, whether they be children, patients, students or clients. The ability to establish, sustain and close relationships requires sensitivity to the subjective, the subtext, as well as any prescribed sets of knowledge and skills.

We recommended a compromise which involves balancing different kinds of assessment evidence. This approach acknowledges the weaknesses of, yet primacy of, judgements. Measurement data is normally translated into grades via value judgements but this is not an error-free process. Atkins et al. (1993) summarised biases associated with the assessment of knowledge acquisition in the following way:

> Certain frames of reference which lecturers bring to assessment are known to bias systematically the way they mark (Heywood, 1989). For example, those who use a 'peer' comparison approach will mark differently from those who are looking for evidence of change in performance since the beginning of the course. These frames of reference may be subconscious and unrecognised and are at their most pernicious in the marking of essay scripts. They may compound other common biases. For example, second markers tend to confirm first marks if they know them, examiners mark down scripts in the middle of a large pile out of fatigue and boredom, and the marks given can be influenced by knowledge of the identity of the candidates. (p. 26)

While the observational strategies used in work settings to elicit and interpret the evidence may appear to be more valid when compared with written assignments, they are equally vulnerable to bias. Rowntree describes the assessment methods of observation, questioning and discussion as being prone to 'all kinds of prejudices, oversights, misinterpretations and idiosyncrasies of standard' (1987, p. 141). These include bias due to racial, cultural or gender stereotypes. The 'halo and horn effects' are common sources of error which involve making the assumption that just because one aspect is good or bad, all will be equally good or bad. Selective perception, first impressions and immediacy may also distort judgements. This is where evidence collection is limited to what the assessor expects, to confirming initial impressions and to the most recent rather than a representative sampling of performance.

Bias can occur as a result of staff–student relationships too. Feelings of like or dislike, of knowing students well from acting as a personal tutor or supervisor, are factors which can also influence assessors' judgements (see Chapters 3 and 4). The conflicting roles of assessor, teacher and counsellor demand clear boundaries to avoid abuse of power.

It is important to acknowledge that analytical and intuitive thinking are complementary (Blomquist, 1985) and that it is necessary to achieve a balance between the two so as to minimise the flaws and maximise the best of each. For example, a gut feeling provides an early warning system which can direct the assessor to obtain evidence to verify or counter this intuition. We believe that a complementary approach may be the most appropriate way of assessing the global components of 'competence to practise', especially the subtle, personal qualities, attitudes and attributes associated with professional unsuitability (see Chapter 2). However, concerns about irresponsibility, unreliability or lack of initiative need to be validated in a systematic way. This can involve documenting examples, collecting the views of others, challenging the student during supervision sessions, recording the feedback given and the action plan agreed, and reviewing change in performance. This ensures the final judgement is based upon sufficient, suitable evidence. Action is the final stage of the assessment cycle. If the assessment is formative the purpose is developmental, whereas if it is summative the outcome is the result – the pass or fail decision. Learning practices and assessment principles should be mutually supportive.

Sufficient, suitable evidence to achieve a pass or fail grade

In the assessment of professional education there is likely to be evidence of both strong and weak areas. It must not be too easy to assume competence and award a pass grade as a default response rather than as an informed decision. Evidence may be elicited via a host of incidental or purposive assessment methods. Each has its own strengths and weaknesses. Some, such as unseen, end-of-course essay and multiple-choice examinations, carry the status of tradition, which often means they are perceived as being more rigorous. Innovative methods, many of which simulate work tasks, have been developed in response to more students in higher education (Gibbs, 1992) and to assess the key skills necessary for employability. These include projects and seminar presentations which are subject to peer, self and tutor assessment.

National Vocational Qualifications are based upon a tight specification of occupational standards. These require the generation, collection and judgement of evidence from the work place. 'The basis of assessment is the generation of evidence by candidates to show that they can achieve the published standards' (Gealy et al., 1990, p. 35). Yet research indicates assessors do not necessarily comply with the assessment guidance which seeks evidence for each element, performance criteria and range. This is because professional judgement intervenes to assure sustainability and consistency of competence from the evidence package as a whole (Raggatt and Hevey, 1995). A similar strategy of 'getting a global impression' followed by systematic reading and reflection is suggested for PhD examiners (Partington et al., 1993).

It is probably impossible to define what constitutes sufficient, suitable evidence because, as with the other principles, it depends upon the context. Assessors need to make choices between different principles. These are likely to be influenced by the interdependence of validity, reliability and the purpose of assessment. Raggatt and Hevey's recommendations about sufficiency are appropriate for most assessments. They state:

'Decisions about sufficiency of evidence are based on the total evidence package. This package should be internally consistent; provide evidence of a candidate's ability to sustain competence including knowledge evidence; include corroborating evidence from different sources and different assessment methods; include evidence that competence on separate functions is fully integrated into the occupational role' (1995, p. 43).

Economy and acceptability

These principles relate to practical considerations, especially the effectiveness, economy and equity of assessment methods. Assessing can be a costly, stressful, time-consuming and complicated administrative exercise. These problems are compounded in work settings where service provision is the priority rather than education or training. There may not be opportunity to gain the required range of experience. Time, equipment and material costs may be prohibitive. Safety risks can prevent a 'hands-on' assessment. An assessment may serve the purpose but be an unacceptable method. For example, performing rectal examinations is an important investigative technique for medical practitioners. Patients are unlikely to provide informed consent to be models for an authentic assessment of students' capability, therefore alternative, technological methods such as mannequins or computer-assisted learning are employed.

Staff need to balance certainty of outcome, costs and ethical considerations when planning an assessment schedule. There are practical constraints on selecting optimal assessment methods. However, Newble et al. suggest 'where compromises between the "ideal" and achievable are made these should be identified explicitly to allow improvement of the assessment procedure in the future' (1994, p. 75). This statement embodies openness, transparency and accountability. These principles reflect government policy in the United Kingdom, a consumer ethos which aims to make explicit the expectations, rights and responsibilities of all stakeholders.

Feedback as part of summative and formative assessment

Another key aspect of good assessment systems relates to students' knowledge of the assessment system, criteria, procedures and feedback mechanisms. It is essential that the explicit assessment standards are understood by all the tutors, students and assessors, but especially by the students as they need to know the outcome standards they are expected to attain. This ensures that students and staff are working towards a shared goal and provides the focus for regular, formative feedback about progress toward the goal. Formative assessment identifies progress as part of an ongoing, developmental process. Students have a right to know how they are doing, to receive an expert opinion about their strengths and weaknesses while working towards the learning outcomes. The feedback needs to be honest and specific in relation to the ways in which their performance meets or does not meet the standards for their particular stage of the course. This is important to avoid any mismatch between the assessor's expectations and stated objectives, especially at an early stage of a programme. Another source of mismatch is when students receive positive feedback to encourage and avoid confronting problems, but it is not a realistic appraisal. In such instances the student is deprived of the opportunity to change and the final, summative assessment can then be an unpleasant shock.

Feedback is necessary along the whole education continuum. It has been identified as a quality indicator in postgraduate medical education. 'The quality of consultant feedback has an important influence on perception of learning, ability to cope and relationships between junior and senior staff' (Baldwin et al., 1997, p. 743). Feedback is a mechanism for learning to 'see ourselves as others see us'. Giving and receiving feedback depends upon qualities such as 'caring, trusting, acceptance, openness and a concern for the needs of others' (Shtogren, 1980, p. 237). It can take a variety of forms from formative, through self and peer to summative assessment.

Several factors are known to influence the effectiveness of feedback. For example, information gathered from a number of credible, knowledgeable and well-intentioned sources (Brinko, 1993). Individuals rely most upon sources close to themselves, especially intrinsic feedback from self and the task (Bastos and Fletcher, 1995). Self-assessment may be considered as the basis for reflection and continued professional development. Realistic appraisal of knowledge and skills is a safety net to prevent practitioners working beyond the bounds of their current abilities. It includes receptivity to feedback from colleagues and service users. This may be at individual performance reviews, appraisals or via ongoing, informal comments.

The timing and content of feedback also influences its effectiveness. Information should be given at the earliest opportunity and as part of a regular process rather than as an isolated event (Brinko, 1993). This supports the value of informal, contemporaneous feedback, regular supervision sessions and a mid-point formative assessment, all of which culminate in a summative assessment. Feedback can be given in a variety of styles – from prescriptive to collaborative – depending upon the purpose and relationship. However, regardless of style, feedback needs to be specific and focused, containing complete, accurate evidence and examples. Feedback is more effective if it focuses upon the behaviour rather than the person, when it is descriptive rather than evaluative, and creates cognitive dissonance. This is to make 'salient the discrepancies between one's self-perceptions and one's ideals and creates a psychological climate that prepares people for change' (Brinko, 1993, p. 580). Choice and change are at the heart of education.

Formative feedback and assessment usually culminate in summative assessments which represent the final judgement of attainment. Summative assessment indicates the achievement of standards with the formal outcome given as a grade, degree classification or certificate of competence. Although these are unidimensional symbols they can hold many meanings (Chapter 1). The same evidence may be interpreted in different ways depending upon the purpose of the assessment – whether it is formative or summative.

Training the trainers

Understanding educational processes would seem to be a logical pre- or co-requisite for those who teach or train, regardless of where this occurs. Yet the evidence suggests subject specialism is assumed to confer this knowledge and skill. For example, Warren-Piper summarised the professionalism of professors as 'there is no requirement for people appointed to academic posts to have any formal education in the processes of teaching and examination with the acquisition of a difficult body of esoteric knowledge. Expertise is, for the most part, developed through on-the-job experience and perhaps, therefore, tends to be pragmatic rather than informed by a body of knowledge' (1994, p. 227). A key reason is the disparity in status between teaching and research in universities. In contrast, the National Council for Vocational Qualifications supported supervisory and assessor qualifications for work-based staff such as those awarded by the Training and Development Lead Bodies. This policy decision was based upon the premise that 'staff training is the normal way of assisting the development of competence … training also requires some form of assessment of performance plus continual monitoring over time to ensure that competence is maintained' (Gealy et al., 1991, p. 48). However, the practical implications – costs, time, bureaucracy and conflict of priorities between work and training – can sabotage these good intentions.

Training trainers (or educators) was one of the recommendations of the Dearing Report (1997) which is being implemented by the new Institute for Teaching and Learning. The proposals include issuing new lecturers with a licence to practise and requiring existing academic staff to attend annual updating courses. However, training comprises more than the process of socialisation described in the Higher Education Quality Council report *Assessment in Higher Education and the Role of 'Graduateness'* (1997). The curriculum needs to cover the obvious and taken for granted to ensure a knowledge-based approach to educational policy, principles and practice. The taken for granted encompasses the transition process (MacNeil, 1997), understanding the conflict in roles and values, the different boundaries for the relationship, and of course, coping with fail scenarios.

Training assessors to apply assessment standards

Earlier in the chapter we stated that good evidence and explicit criteria are two essential components of a good assessment system. The third is training so that all assessors are fully conversant with the assessment standards, principles and procedures. Unfortunately, there is an assumption that some staff, by virtue of their experience as practitioners or professional educators, possess a highly developed sense of how to assess students. This, of course, is highly dangerous logic as an expert practitioner is not automatically a good assessor of others' practice. The problems are compounded because assessment criteria are often difficult to illustrate through written guidance alone.

This is why training opportunities are needed so staff can explore the exemplification of outcome standards in real assessment situations. Although there is no simple, single formula for planning such training, it is desirable if it simulates assessment practice. Encouraging discussions about assessment criteria and procedures is better than no training at all, but getting assessors to apply these in the context of judging actual student performance is more likely to reveal problems or training needs. In supportive, learning contexts judgments can be compared with peers and discrepancies investigated in relation to the agreed assessment criteria. We believe that assessment is far too an important topic to be restricted to one-off training events. Assessors, however experienced, should be given regular opportunities to have their assessment standards reviewed. In the very best professional education systems, moderation and standardisation procedures ensure that all assessors receive regular feedback on their assessment standards. Acquiring the skills to allow one to become an expert assessor of professional education involves a set of complicated decision processes. These need to be refined, retuned and closely monitored throughout an assessor's career because the assessment procedures and criteria will change in line with developments in professional practice.

The highly specialist topic of dealing with student failures in professional education also needs to be covered in assessment training courses. In Chapter 4 we discussed the stress that failing may cause, not only for the student, but also for others. Assessors can benefit from preparation to help them confront and handle these situations well (Ilott, 1995). Such training is essential to support assessors so they do not 'just pass' or give marginal students the 'benefit of the doubt' because they cannot deal with the consequences of giving a fail grade. An assessor who is unable or unwilling to fail a student in professional education is really not any use as an assessor. Although this is a strong statement we make it because such staff are incapable of performing a core function of an assessor. Neither the assessor nor the assessment system or educational institution has any credibility if student success is guaranteed regardless of the evidence produced.

Good principles provide a sound foundation for fail scenarios

We believe assessors need to understand assessment principles if they are to become effective educationalists as well as subject experts. Assessment of competence and conduct is complicated. It encompasses the triad of fitness to practise, for purpose and award. This demands judgement. The challenge is to devise valid, integrated assessments which are reliable, practicable, economical and acceptable. Sufficient evidence needs to be obtained from a range of sources. The evidence is then evaluated on the 'balance of probabilities' or 'beyond reasonable doubt', depending upon whether it is a first or final fail.

While the framework for a good assessment system will be tailored to the requirements and opportunities of each professional education programme, they are likely to incorporate the key features introduced in this chapter. Even though the practice of assessing students will vary for different professional groups, it should revolve around the collection of quality evidence, the application of clear and agreed criteria, assessor training and robust mechanisms for student feedback. Without this foundation, the system will probably be unable to meet the challenges explored in this book.

Any system is likely to require a compromise between the ideal principles summarised in this chapter and the constraints of the real situation, which include institutional and personal inertia about change. There will probably always be conflicts between time and competing priorities from the Research Assessment Exercise to service commitments in work settings. But good principles offer support in worst-case scenarios. Students are challenging consumers of education. Paying for the privilege results in ownership. Good principles can offer some degree of self-protection. They give examiners the assurance of making the right decision – based on the best evidence.

Chapter 6
Applying the assessment cycle to fail scenarios

Introduction

The good assessment practices summarised in the previous chapter provide the basis for devising appropriate strategies for coping with failure in academic and practice settings. In this chapter these principles are applied along a continuum from making the assessment decisions, through informing the students, to coping with any aftermath when the fail grade has been given. The assessment cycle of eliciting, interpreting and acting on the evidence gives the structure to these general guidelines. They are not prescriptive. This is because each situation is different and assessors must modify and make the principles appropriate to their circumstances. The whole process – from heeding alarm bells, through feedback and listening skills, to coping with an appeal – is reviewed. All aspects are interdependent and depend upon the courage to make good judgements.

Quality decision making, which involves weighing all the evidence of competence and incompetence, is important so decisions are based 'on the balance of probabilities' or 'beyond reasonable doubt' (Gonczi, 1994). The latter is particularly important for a final fail which results in withdrawal from a training course. If there is a student appeal, the assessor needs to be certain and to justify their judgement with sufficient, suitable documented evidence as this helps to 'prove' both the appropriateness of the result and fairness of the process. Staff must avoid educational malpractice for the 'failure to instruct properly (which includes passing a failing student and failing a passing student) may be a negligent act' (Goclowski, 1985, p. 107).

Decision making

This first stage of the assessment cycle can be marked by anticipatory anxiety and self-doubt (Chapter 4). This is because decision making involves thinking the unthinkable. Often, intuitive alarm bells give a forewarning. Concerns need to be substantiated or refuted by eliciting purposive and incidental evidence, interpreting this against clear bench-marks and obtaining second opinions. Simultaneously, action in the form of formative assessment with unambiguous feedback and suggestions for change should be offered to ensure the student receives 'due process'.

Listening to the alarm bells

Openness to cues and inklings of concern is essential from the start. Such sensitivity represents a responsiveness to intuitive, subjective factors which can act as alarm signals. These may be activated early, often within the first few days. It is easy to dismiss these suspicions, especially if asses-sors assume all students possess the requisite level of competence, commitment, personal and professional qualities. This is just a supposi-tion which needs to be tested by gathering evidence of both competence and incompetence. A willingness to believe the unbelievable was one of the most important lessons of the Allitt Inquiry (1994).

Early recognition of potential problems raises the question of whether students should start with 'a clean sheet, a clean record' or whether the assessor should receive information about their past achievements and problems. Opinion is divided. Some prefer prior knowledge so they are able to provide assistance and know the answer to the question 'is history repeating itself?' Others prefer to judge for themselves, to eliminate precon-ceived ideas and any self-fulfilling prophecy. Cohen and Blumberg (1991) describe this as 'one of the unresolved controversies in education' (p. 288). They conclude a review in medical education with the recommendation: 'Problems encountered in the student's mastery of academic content or procedural skills, attitudes and other personal qualities and interactive skills and personal health should be shared with subsequent faculty. Students must be central to the entire process...[they] should be encouraged to initiate the process' (p. 289). This recommendation balances the student's right to confidentiality, emphasises the importance of awareness and responsibility in the change process, and reduces the distorting effect of the 'unofficial grapevine'. It is certainly a fixed principle within good systems that assessment information should be carried forward to be developed and amended in a way which informs the progress of the individual. The 'fresh start' philosophy has in our view been overplayed in many settings as a way of excusing poor assessment systems. It can inhibit the transfer and appro-priate use of student records, which within good assessment systems are a valuable resource for informing learning if shared with future assessors.

Eliciting and interpreting the evidence

A suspicion should then be substantiated or refuted by evidence. The student has a right to be treated fairly, to be judged beyond reason-able doubt and not to be condemned by negative first impressions. The collection of sound evidence from a range of impartial and informed sources is also a support strategy to combat self-doubt. Self interrogation – such as 'Is it me or is it them?', 'Are my expectations too high?', 'Why hasn't anyone else noticed this before?', 'What haven't I done?', 'Is it my fault?', 'Am I experienced enough?', 'Am I competent to judge?', 'How might a fail grade damage the student?' – provokes anxiety, undermines confidence and can sabotage decision making.

Work-based supervisors are advised to contact the higher education institution at this early stage to alert them to a potential problem. Academic staff should be able to provide a more objective, informed reply to the self-doubt and interrogation. Such communication allows work-practice organisers to schedule an early visit, to reassure the practitioner, to probe their concerns, and to compile a profile from other work-based and academic settings to suggest alternative supervisory strategies. Work-placement staff may be reluctant, perceiving initiating contact as an admission of failure. It is not. It is a rational response to a concern which is best shared with academic colleagues at an early stage.

Types of evidence and reference level

Purposive and incidental evidence should be elicited, interpreted, discussed and documented throughout the assessment cycle. Purposive evidence may be collected in response to the alarm. This involves the assessor designing a task to test the student's knowledge or capabilities. It can be formal or informal and include probing questions, observation, a written assignment or practical task. Incidental evidence is elicited spontaneously and continuously. It may provide 'evidence of deeper understanding than being able to apply that particular skill when being told to do so' (Wiliam and Black, 1996).

Incidental evidence in work settings is elicited as an appropriate response to a particular client or situation. It possesses high ecological validity but is vulnerable to misinterpretation because the evidence is ephemeral, impossible to replay or be verified by others. The same evidence may be interpreted in different ways by the same or different assessors at different times. This is the nub of concerns about inter-rater and test–retest reliability. This is why a reference level is so important. The reference level is the benchmark, representing what is normally expected at this stage in an educational programme. As such it ensures procedural consistency, fairness and constancy of performance criteria. The reference level may be stated with different degrees of specificity in learning outcomes, aims and objectives, criterion-referenced statements, marking guidelines and assessment criteria. Academic staff usually set the reference level in relation to the curriculum. It is then likely to be tailored to the context (with specific outcomes which match the opportunities available in a work setting) and the experience, aspirations and interests of the student via an individual learning plan or contract.

A clear reference level is particularly valuable for new assessors because they lack a reserve of experience to compare the performance of the current student with others at a similar stage of training. Assessment requires fine judgements, whether about honours classification or competence to practise. Comparability and consistency of such judgements are difficult, but even more so without a reference level. Recently, the diversity of degrees was considered analogous to a range of cars – with different types for different purposes. The Higher Education Quality Council's two-year Graduate Standards Programme (1997) acknowledged this diversity and was unable to guarantee a comparable standard of degrees awarded by United Kingdom higher education institutions.

There can be added difficulties when considering a reference level for a fail or borderline pass–fail grade. Although there seems to be an unspoken consensus about the knowledge, skills and attitudes which constitute a fail grade in vocational programmes (Chapter 2), this may conflict with the criteria for some third class honours degrees. For example, to achieve a grade of 40–49 per cent the work would 'miss key points, contain important inaccuracies, assertions not supported by authority or evidence' (HEQC, 1997). This definition is inappropriate for professional courses because it does not reflect the demands of fitness for purpose or practice (Chapter 2). Feelings can also sabotage decision making, especially anxiety, guilt and fear of the student's reaction (see Chapter 4). Fail grades are infrequent in academic settings and rare in work settings. This means even experienced assessors may not have encountered a fail scenario, even vicariously, if the subject is not included on teaching or supervisory courses.

Verification and support from others

Verification means offering the evidence to others to confirm or disagree with your interpretation. This can take a variety of forms: external examiners as impartial, independent subject experts appointed by the university to monitor a particular programme, scrutinise purposive evidence – all the assessment material at the end of a semester, academic level or programme. Incidental evidence may be verified informally by listening to the views of the service users – the clients, patients or students. The principle of triangulation is useful to apply when collecting, collating and synthesising the evidence. This means obtaining information from different sources and by different methods to obtain a complete picture and so reduce bias or personality clashes.

Second opinions

There is much reassurance when your judgement is confirmed by a respected other person. Seeking a second opinion also protects the student and staff from the possibility of a personality clash. This tactic was commended by Pope (1983), who noted that the courts in the USA comment approvingly when supervisory observations are documented by written anecdotal comments and supported by additional observations from other competent assessors.

A second and third opinion, through internal moderation and external examining, is an intrinsic part of most academic systems. Group decision making usually encompasses informal staff discussion to formal examination boards which ratify the result. Implicit assessment constructs and incidental evidence may be a feature of informal discussion. These include the students' profile of performance throughout the whole course, whether they 'deserve to fail', attendance and professional behaviour, and possible grounds for an appeal.

Recent reviews of the external examiner system highlight the variability of practice and near impossibility of assuring comparable standards in the new, modular and semesterised mass higher education industry (Higher Education Quality Council 1994; Silver 1993). Although the system is under strain and subject to criticism it seems to be valued in the extraordinary circumstances of fails. External examiners are seen as impartial, external agents who offer an objective, independent perspective. They were described as 'vital' by a course leader because 'they give a dispassionate view from the intense emotional atmosphere which happens in school. They are objective and fair to the student.' This quotation illustrates the dangers of subjectivity, especially when 'liking' a student threatens to jeopardise threshold standards. Green (1991) condemns the special sort of relationship which verges on collusion. There is emotional distance between a student and external examiner. The decision is made by weighing the purposive evidence against a reference level. An experienced external examiner described it as 'impersonal. It has to be. You are not dealing with the intricacies of the person. I am not failing a person but a candidate with a number who could not get the facts straight.'

External examiners usually act as the final arbiters by signing the pass list at the examination board. However, there are different perceptions about this role. There can be conflict when external examiners raise or lower the internal assessor's marks. Ilott's (1993) study revealed two approaches for handling this: autonomy and delegation – the choice depending upon the experience and attitude of the manager (head of school, course leader or programme director). Autonomy means responsibility is retained within the staff group. Double and triple marking are used to agree the outcome in advance. In contrast, delegation involved offering recommendations to the external examiners and then 'abiding by their decision'. This parallels the delegation to work-based assessors who are expected to accept full, personal and direct responsibility for assigning a fail grade, but without the organisational support available in a higher education establishment. While such mechanisms do not reduce the distance or trauma for academic staff they do provide 'reassuring confirmation and validation of your judgement' (lecturer).

Second opinions are equally important for work-based assessors. There are stark differences between the collective and anonymous academic procedures and the personal, face-to-face, direct judgements and continuous contact in work settings. Greater reliance upon incidental evidence, the one-to-one supervisory relationship with less opportunities for comparison or verification, all make work-based assessments extra difficult. This means alternative arrangements, either existing or one-off, need to be made to ensure fail grades are a team rather an individual decision, even in community settings. Such arrangements may include informal consultation with peers or as part of a split placement (between different work-based settings or supervisors). Line managers can contribute through supervision and support. A supervisor reported how these intra-professional networks provide 'a fair, objective second opinion'. The views of other members of the multidisciplinary team and support workers may also be sought about overall impressions or specific concerns. Another source of evidence is the opinion, feedback and reactions of the service users. They are customers and consumers of the service provided by the student. The principle of triangulating the evidence from different sources to obtain a complete, comprehensive picture is applicable to work placements too.

Work-practice organisers, where they exist, are another source of background information and support. These are academic staff who straddle the academic and work-based components of the course. They highlight the interrelationship between theory and practice through having access to both environments 'but without really belonging to either'(work-practice organiser). The role of work-practice organisers may be compared with that of external examiners. They are influential, external agents who oversee the assessment process. However, they may be perceived as less objective or impartial because they are employees of the higher education establishment. Their role is to provide support to both supervisor and student. Work-practice organisers act as an independent adviser, giving advice on alternative supervisory strategies and information about regulations, procedures and paperwork. Supervisors describe their role as 'extremely supportive...we were thinking in terms of problems but she crystallised it into failure', and 'she gave us the confidence to acknowledge there was a problem and that is wasn't me. This helped relieve our guilt. She looked at the whole situation and helped the student too.' This quotation parallels the intentions of a work-practice organiser: 'I aim to be fair and see the situation from the outside.'

However, giving permission to award a fail grade does not always work. The following example from a work-practice organiser summarises the difficulties: 'Supervisors allow themselves to get into difficult situations because they do not have clear learning outcomes, or they do not provide honest feedback. They are being therapists to the student. Towards the end of the placement they realise there is a real problem. The student has been given good grades for encouragement but they have not improved. They have not got any evidence on which to base a lower grade. The supervisor is trapped. So the student is allowed to pass.' This quotation leads into the next stage of the assessment cycle – evidence should be used to inform action via formative and summative assessments.

Giving honest, formative feedback

Action should be the natural sequel which follows the elicitation and inter-pretation of the evidence. As the above quotation suggests, however, giving candid, unambiguous feedback can be difficult. Yet it is the assessor's responsibility to do so. If not, the student is deprived of 'due process' or the opportunity to improve. This section focuses on formative assessment and feedback which culminates in a judgement about compe-tence. Summative assessment represents a synthesis of the all the purpo-sive and incidental evidence of attainment and aptitude. An important component is the students' response to feedback, their insight and ability to learn from mistakes, their willingness and capacity to change. A refusal or inability to do so is a criterion for awarding a fail grade (Chapter 2). Yet using the fail word is difficult. Softer phrases such as 'not quite there' and 'you need to improve' tend to be preferred so as not to discourage the student or distress the staff. However, these euphemisms do not seem to work. They can obscure, defer or avoid necessary decisions. It is important to remember that with the vision of hindsight, the failure to fail causes most regret and guilt.

Effective feedback is specific, containing detailed evidence about strengths, weaknesses and advice about how to overcome the problems. This means identifying what students can do, giving praise for what they do well, clearly stating what they are doing wrong, discussing the reasons for these difficulties, giving advice, guidelines and instructions about what they must do differently. Specificity is essential. This means using examples from a range of situations, sources and seriousnesses to illus-trate particular points during the meeting. Frankness is also required. The consequences of non-compliance must be understood: failure to change will mean a fail grade. While self-assessment and exploration is likely to be a feature of most supervisory sessions, it is important to establish that judgements about threshold standards are non-negotiable.

Contemporaneous records which document the feedback are impor-tant. They are likely to contain a record of formative feedback, of regular supervision sessions and particular untoward incidents. The record may include the specific problems, learning goals and strategies to improve performance with warnings about the seriousness of the concerns. The 'fail' word needs to be used – both during discussions and in the documentation – to help those who lack insight, or do not wish to hear, appreciate the reality of the situation. Awareness is the starting point for change or a reappraisal of career choice. The record should be understood, signed and dated by the assessor and student. It may then be reviewed at the next meeting when improvements are noted, continuing or new difficulties added and future steps agreed. Such a progress record gives a profile with plateaux and peaks of good or poor performance. This allows patterns to be identified and substantiated, for causes to be understood in the context of explanations offered or situations encountered. Such documentation provides evidence when considering 'the balance of probabilities' and 'beyond reasonable doubt'. It also shows that the student has been treated fairly and the assessors have fulfilled their supervisory responsibilities. This is essential to combat feelings of guilt and self-doubt, especially 'Is it them or is it me?' and 'Have I done enough?'

The provision of specific, candid and documented feedback is an overarching assessment principle. Yet expressing what may be the equivalent of bad news is difficult, especially for those from the caring professions because it conflicts with their humanistic values. The conflict can be reduced if feedback is constructive, if it concentrates upon the tasks to be performed and does not undermine the person. Formative assessment is developmental, and as such it should assist not inhibit learning. The following pointers, derived from the literature and research, are intended to enhance the learning value of feedback.

When giving feedback:

- Start and end with the positive. Most people need encouragement and appreciate praise and being told when they are meeting expectations, achieving or exceeding the required standard. External feedback supports intrinsic motivation. It counters the impression 'I can't do anything right', which can spiral into negativity and become self-fulfilling. Valuing what the student can do and is doing well also demonstrates concern for the person. Students are also likely to be able to take constructive criticism much better if it is given in a context where they have already been affirmed and praised.
- Be specific. Avoid general comments such as 'It was awful' which do not indicate what was wrong or what is required. Such global comments about overall performance are too vague to be helpful. They need to be supported by evidence, examples and critical incidents. Complex tasks can be analysed into their component parts so the particular problem is identified. In this way the feedback is based on accurate data, concrete information, complete and irrefutable evidence. The content also needs to be tailored to the individual and not be generalised to 'most students'.
- Refer to behaviour which can be changed. It is inappropriate to comment on factors which are beyond the student's control. For example, 'I don't like your face' is rude, destructive feedback. To be constructive there

must be possibility of change: 'You need to look at people when you speak, to maintain eye contact so you can watch their reaction. If you do not, you seem disinterested.' This statement offers alternative behaviour: what could be done differently and why. It provides the basis for a practical action plan which can be monitored by the student and others. The reference is more useful if it is descriptive rather than just evaluative. It reduces defensiveness which impairs 'hearing the message'. This means the statement goes beyond 'that was bad' to what was observed and the effect it had on the assessor. For example, 'Your tone of voice as you spoke really made me feel as though you were concerned.' These pointers offer information which the student can choose to accept or reject. They do not demand change but state the consequences of action or inaction in terms of the immediate interaction and for the summative assessment. The student is encouraged to make an informed choice based on explicit assessment criteria. This allows the student to take responsibility for their own learning and failing.

- Own the feedback. The feedback will be more convincing if it is owned through the use of 'I' and reinforced through non-verbal communication. The earlier examples use 'I' to demonstrate the power of the personal pronoun. The examiner is offering expert opinion which may be verified by others. It also avoids the impression of being the giver of cosmic, critical judgements about everything from everyone. The verbal message will be more effective if it is supported, not contradicted, via non-verbal methods. These include body posture, tone of voice, eye contact and gesture. It is important to convey confidence, assertiveness and concern. If doubt or hesitancy are communicated non-verbally then the student will receive mixed messages or the wrong message. Authentic motives are needed for convincing, constructive feedback.

- Give selective, timely feedback. A focus is important, rather than covering all problems at once. The topics may be selected according to priority, risk or consequences. Immediate knowledge of results is most useful. If known, feedback should be immediate and not delayed, especially if this is a way of avoiding a confrontation. The assessor needs to be able to disentangle effort and ability (Chapter 4). It is easier to recognise and praise effort, allowing interest to compensate for a lack of minimum standards, rather than vice versa. Feedback should focus on the reference level as the critical component of competence.

- Remember self-evaluation can provide a starting point. Feedback is more effective when information is gathered from oneself as well as from others. It can remind the assessor of the student's experience and stage of training. Realistic self-appraisal is a routine, professional expectation. Recognising the limits of your knowledge and skills is essential for safe practice (chapter two). It is a prerequisite for continued professional development.

- Check that the message has been received and understood. Listening to negative feedback is not easy. It may be received with disinterest and apathy as a denial mechanism. Another problematic response is lack of insight. The student may not acknowledge, and certainly may not own, that there is as problem: that knowledge, skills, attitudes or aptitudes are below the minimum acceptable standard. It is important to test their understanding, to check that he or she has understood what has been said. This may be done by asking the student to repeat what has been heard, agreement or disagreement with the interpretation of the evidence, and about similar previous feedback. Such paraphrasing, summarising and recall is an important part of the dialogue. It is essential to maintain channels of communication at a difficult time because it helps to convey concern. Feedback is well intentioned when it is offered to facilitate learning rather than punish. Engaging the student in the debate encourages self-evaluation, reflection and appraisal. This can be done by inviting him or her to think about and specify what can be done differently and describe how to know whether the change has been effective. Finally, ask the student to conjecture about the consequences of acting or ignoring the feedback. These open-ended, probing questions give the assessor an inside view, helping them to understand the meaning of the fail grade. It may even be welcome as a wanted way out of a wrong career choice.
- Maintain boundaries. Fears and feelings can erode professional and personal boundaries. The book has emphasised how feelings may sabotage decision making. This is related to a fundamental conflict in values and roles between being a caring professional, developing strengths and setting threshold standards as an examiner. Making judgements and being judgmental can be such an antithesis that it is avoided. Another reason for avoidance is the fear of confrontation and coping with the students' unpredictable responses. These can range from anger to distress and denial. Even so, it is important to maintain personal and professional boundaries. These include differentiating between failure as a person and on a task, remembering the difference between teaching and learning, and respecting the professional obligation to maintain future standards.

A useful strategy is to ask yourself 'what are the consequences of not giving feedback?' Most importantly, the student is deprived of the opportunity to change. Also, the feelings are likely to fester and interfere with the student–staff relationship. A supervisor described this experience: 'Confronting is better than letting it bubble up inside. It is better if the fail is out in the open, to be honest with the student in a constructive way. If it is left to fester it will come out in different, less constructive ways. But you need courage to confront it.' Students are unlikely to be insensitive to a negative appraisal, even if it is only expressed via non-verbal leakage.

Kagan and Albertson (1987) suggest students are 'hypersensitive to any criticism of their performance' (p. 57). Negative feedback, if conveyed by a credible, knowledgeable and well-intentioned source, can be valued. 'Subjects who received more credible negative feedback set higher goals and performed tasks at higher levels that those who received less credible negative feedback' (Brinko, 1993, p. 577).

Feedback, whether formative or summative, is vital for learning. The ability to give honest, helpful feedback without belittling is consistently rated as a characteristic of good teachers, supervisors and quality learning environments (Baldwin et al., 1997; Cameron and Wilson, 1993; Chesser and Brett, 1989; Nehring, 1990). Students have a right to receive prompt, detailed feedback in both academic and work settings. Negative feedback can be difficult to articulate and sensitive information may be conveyed at a cost to the assessor. This was summarised by a supervisor: 'At the end of the day the student would go but we would stay till 6.00 pm catching up, clearing up and report writing. It took longer to do the student's weekly report. We were careful about the wording, trying to find something positive and to be truthful.'

Yet giving, documenting and then reviewing the student's response to feedback and ability and willingness to change all critical components of the decision-making stage. To be effective feedback must be honest, even though this can be difficult. People tend to be reluctant to deliver unambiguous negative feedback. It is more likely to be positive or inscrutable. But such feedback may be collusive, not developmental, because 'people are apparently predisposed to interpret ambiguous feedback as positive feedback' (Snyder and Higgins, 1988, p. 31), which then reduces the learning value of the information.

Feedback should be the starting point for action which may include choosing priorities, agreeing learning objectives, how they will be achieved (methods, resources and facilities to support study skills or performance), when they will be reviewed and assessed. Action planning should also be based upon explicit assessment constructs so the student knows exactly what they are expected to know or do.

Explicit assessment constructs

The student has a right to know the criteria, standards or baseline against which they are judged. Such benchmarks may be expressed in varying ways. These range from syllabi which list essential knowledge, skills and attitudes; through behavioural or process objectives as learning outcomes which state what the student will be able to do; to detailed occupational standards which specify the performance requirements in the workplace. Explicit assessment constructs are important because they provide the reference level which supports the validity and reliability of the whole process.

However, Ilott (1993) and other studies such as Alexander (1996) indicate assessors also use implicit assessment constructs. This means official, formal standards are supplemented by personal criteria. Alexander (1996) describes how physiotherapy work-based assessors may estimate students' ability from a general impression of their performance and that the grade can be influenced by the students' personality. Chapter 2 revealed how infrequently occupational therapy supervisors use the institutionally sanctioned objectives and report forms when making pass–fail decisions. Academic assessors also report using similar global criteria. These include the student's potential to be a good practitioner, their employability and professional suitability. Effort is another important implicit criterion. It comprises interest, hard work, response to feedback and signs of improvement. Assessors seem to want to reward effort with a pass grade, even when the threshold standard has not been reached. Lack of effort tends to be associated with professional unsuitability.

Although implicit criteria can benefit and penalise students we do not condone their use. This is because implicit criteria are random, unequal and ultimately unfair. An explicit reference level means the decision-making process is open and accountable. Appropriate evidence is collected, interpreted and acted upon via regular, documented feedback, the assessment criteria are understood by both student and assessor. This makes justice to the student more likely. Weighing the evidence of competence and incompetence, using second opinions for verification, are important safeguards. They allow staff to demonstrate to themselves and others (whether student or appeals board) that they made fair decisions on the basis of clear, explicit criteria. This gives the confidence and courage necessary for the next stage when decisions are transformed into action.

Final report- or results-giving meeting

Action is the logical outcome of assessment. The previous section focused on formative assessment which fulfils a developmental purpose through feedback, practice and review. The final, summative assessment has a different purpose. This involves a judgement about attainment – whether the gap between actual and the threshold level of competence has been closed. If not, the result is a fail grade. The consequences for career plans from a summative assessment are very different from formative assessments. This is why the judgement needs to be based upon the highest standard of proof, i.e. 'beyond reasonable doubt'. This requires a high degree of probability – the assessor is 'satisfied so that they are sure'. This does not mean that the proof is 'beyond the shadow of a doubt', as this is impossible to achieve.

This section focuses upon managing the meeting/s at which the results are conveyed, confirmed and discussed. There are significant variations between final meetings held in work placement and academic ettings; whether it is a first or final fail which requires withdrawal from the training; and the relationship between the giver and receiver of the information. In work settings the summative report is usually the culmination of many formative assessments. This means that the outcome is likely to be known. The fail grade is confirmed officially at this final meeting when the grade is entered on the report form. The result may also be already known in academic settings. This may be via the posting of pass lists on notice boards, or in personally addressed envelopes collected or posted following ratification by the examination board. Ilott's (1993) study revealed how some managers circumvent these impersonal, formal and bureaucratic procedures. They telephone the student immediately after the examination board to inform them of the results, and are available for a number of meetings (both pre and post the examination board) which may include the student's partner or family. This was because 'I think failure is devastating for the student. I therefore spend time with them considering their life options.'

We offer some examples of bad practice as a warning about the failure to fail. A work-practice organiser described feeling angry when 'supervisors pull back from making the final decision. The students cannot redeem themselves in the last week. They have been pressurised by the student via bullying or emotional blackmail.' Such avoidance damages the reputation of the supervisor: 'I am disappointed if a student passes when he or she should fail. I am careful about using the supervisor again. I am less likely to trust their judgement and would only place "safe" students with them.' Perhaps the most damaging example is when the assessor refuses to exercise their professional obligation. This scenario was reported by a manager: 'We had a final pass report from a placement but then the supervisor sent a separate letter saying the student should not be doing occupational therapy. We asked for documentation so we could confront the student. The supervisor replied they had given all the information to the student who had not, or could not, assimilate it. Therefore they had passed a very weak student.' Unjustly passing is far more pernicious than justly failing as it constitutes education malpractice.

Avoidance of the appropriate words and action following summative assessments seems to be common throughout education. For example, *Reporting Pupil's Achievement*, a study on written reports from 222 nursery, primary and secondary schools conducted by the Office of Standards in Education, concluded that 'more than half of the reports to parents in all years fail to diagnose weakness in the pupils' understanding and skills in curriculum subjects, and thus fail to make it clear what the pupil has to do to improve' (Preston, 1995). In the same year, a reluctance to make frank judgements was noted at the other end of the education spectrum. The Royal Society of Chemistry, in a report entitled *The Chemistry PhD: The Enhancement of its Quality*, state: 'Failure by some institutions to apply sufficiently rigorous standards has drawn adverse comments from industry. The apparent reluctance of some supervisors and some universities to require students who are not coping with the rigours of a PhD programme to re-register...or...discontinue their studies, is not compatible with the need to maintain the standard of the PhD award, nor in the best interest of the individual student' (Irwin, 1995).

Concern for the best interests of the student, but within the context of professional responsibilities, is a key strategy for coping with and during a final meeting. This stage will be considered using the framework of the 'five As' from *Tough Interviews* (Hodson, 1993). The As are: anticipation, announcement, anger, acceptance and action. This framework was developed for line managers coping with sensitive situations – discipline, poor performance and redundancy – (Keys and Henshall, 1990; Stewart and Stewart, 1982). It is supplemented by information on how to break bad news in medicine (Buckman and Kason, 1992) and from the research into the assessors' perspective on failing students (Ilott, 1993). The five As provide the structure because they do not assume a fail grade is 'bad news'. The perception depends upon how the student (and others) interpret this unidimensional symbol. Multiple meanings are possible. The range of student reactions are also described in the section on anger.

Anticipation

Anticipation is preparing for the final meeting. Again, there are variations depending upon the setting and role of staff members. The exit interview may be conducted by the manager. Anticipation is usually a two-stage process comprising confirmation of the decision and preparing for the interview. Confirmation includes gathering accurate information about the failure and the student's overall performance from documentation and staff; checking the fairness of and agreement with the decision; seeking clarification and investigating any doubts. A manager described this stage as 'exploring thoroughly, so I am not muddled, to unravel all the parts'. The second stage of preparation encompasses practical and emotional elements. Attention to procedural details, to check the assessment regulations have been adhered to and there have not been any irregularities which could give rise to a student appeal, are important. It also provides assurance 'of the justice and facts of the situation so I am able to demonstrate these to the student'.

Time is valued so the manager can reflect, rehearse and think about the student's possible emotional response. Also, to secure the availability of relevant colleagues, such as the personal/pastoral tutor, subject specialist or work-practice organiser. This is to 'make sure that there is no room for error, misunderstandings, being unclear or saying different things to different people'. Time is required to prepare the papers and room, to create a safe environment – a quiet, comfortable, uncluttered venue without interruptions or distractions.

Confirmation and preparation also apply when other staff are conveying, confirming and discussing failed academic or work-based assessments. A lecturer repeated the need for time 'to consider how I am going to deal with it, sort out potential student responses, my feelings and how I will react'. Work-practice organisers reported using managers/ course leaders for personal and procedural advice, reassurance and guidance 'at all stages. To check examination policies. This checking and sharing of responsibility is important to prevent getting side-tracked.' Support from work-practice organisers, line managers and colleagues was an essential element of preparation for supervisors. This comprised reassurance, understanding and confirmation by those familiar with the situation. It also shows concern for due process, reduces the risk of subjectivity or a personality clash (Meisenhelder, 1982) and 'demonstrates to the student that there is a genuine interest in giving a fair evaluation' (Brozenec et al., 1987).

A final practical point is the timing of the meeting – day of the week and time of the day. The meeting may be open-ended as the duration is unpredictable depending upon the student's response. Time needs to be given for a debriefing afterwards. Another factor to take into consideration is the availability of support for the student at the end. This may be provided by peers, their personal tutor or student counsellors, for example. Some assessors avoid giving final reports on Fridays and late afternoons so the student is not left alone after the meeting.

Pre-meeting preparation involves logistical points such as organising the time, room, papers and staff. The exit interview is usually conducted by two people. For example, the manager or work-place supervisor is accompanied by the student's personal tutor, work-practice organiser or line manager. This may be for mutual support, to prevent manipulation and a change of outcome, or misinterpretation afterwards. It also provides an opportunity for learning through debriefing. Readiness is a prerequisite for the next phase: announcement.

Announcement

Announcement is communicating the fail grade. The discussion may include informing, confirming and justifying the outcome. In academic settings results will usually have been conveyed in writing to individuals or the cohort. The summative report giving meeting should be the culmination of the regular, formative supervision sessions in work settings. As such, the result is unlikely to be a surprise. Also, students are more than capable of self-assessment, evaluating and comparing their performance with their peers, and calculating their grade point averages.

This stage needs to be characterised by clear communication to maintain the educational relationship. Staff have a duty to convey distressing news with compassion, not in a careless manner. This involves straight talk. A fail must be called a fail. This means the student has not reached the required standard on academic- or practice-based assignments. It does not mean that they are a failed, useless or worthless person. The fail grade and the consequences (retake assessments or withdrawal from the programme) is best stated clearly, simply and briefly at the start of the meeting. Procrastination is unnecessary and unhelpful. Non-verbal communication should reinforce the verbal message. The following example from a work-practice organiser illustrates how gesture, posture and eye contact can support the verbal interaction: 'I change posture to reflect and reiterate the problems. I adopt a relaxed posture when it is quiet and calm. Important statements are anchored with gestures, eye contact and asking the student to repeat what they have heard. I monitor the latent and linguistic content, the choice of vocabulary and metaphor, what is said and what is left unsaid.'

Listening and attending skills are especially important. Irrespective of whether the fail grade is known or unexpected, confirmation is likely to be shock. The student may not be able or willing to hear any more information. Details, either to justify or explain the result, are often best left until another meeting. Silence may be uncomfortable but listening, giving the student time to talk, to express their anger, sadness or relief, is essential. Announcement, therefore, consists of communicating the news – 'You have failed the assessment for the second time. According to the examination rules this means you cannot continue on the programme' – then listening and responding.

Anger

The unpredictability of the students' reaction is a major source of anticipatory anxiety for assessors. The final interview, whether conducted in an academic or work setting, is a private, confidential encounter. Ilott's (1993) study explored how students do react to a fail grade and the most difficult response for assessors. A whole gamut of emotional reactions depending upon the person and reason were reported – not just anger. This is because the meaning (both for the giver and receiver) depends upon 'a series of constantly shifting personal and situational frames of reference' (Pollio et al., 1988, p. 155). The types of meaning – social, trait, personal and procedural (Pollio et al, 1989) – described in Chapter 1 will influence a student's reaction. Wilson (1972) reported 'three common reactions to failure – equanimity, resentment or guilt' (p. 31). These reactions can be understood within the framework of personal and social meanings whereas attribution theory only predicts shame from lack of ability and guilt from lack of effort (Hunter and Barker, 1987).

Tears and anger were the most frequently reported responses. Distress – 'devastated and inconsolable' – was an expected response. Disappointment was expressed 'even though they may be expecting it...they hope they will pass regardless of all the feedback to the contrary'. Anger – 'she was very verbally aggressive, abusive' – was unexpected and, for the least experienced, the most difficult reaction to cope with. The third most frequent response was acceptance. This incorporated agreement with the decision and relief. One supervisor described the 'physical transformation, the relief from lifting the burden of having to continue on an unwanted course'. Such responses contradict negative stereotypes. Also, it may reflect a realistic self-appraisal, for, as Boekaerts (1991) reports, a person's self efficacy can determine how much effort he or she is willing to persist in the face of obstacles and aversive experience. A range of passive and active reactions were described, including being subdued, giving no reaction, expressing bewilderment and being impassive; active reactions covered 'bolting, running away', threatening to use the appeal system and 'attempting blackmail with their questions. Am I sure? Have I been fair? Will I explain myself?'

Reactions may change over time, mirroring shifts in personal and situational meanings. The next examples for a first fail in academic and work settings show the interaction between student responses and staff feelings of effectiveness. 'The best is when they arrive in tears, accept the fail and leave smiling. This is how students respond the majority of times. They are grateful for advice so they can avoid a second fail' (lecturer). 'Initially she was very tearful. This was OK because we could handle this. But when she came back a month later she was angry, hostile, blaming us and trying to off-load responsibility on to us by saying "I've never had any problems on other placements". This made us feel like ogres' (work-based supervisor). This would seem to be an excuse attribution which involves blaming others or the difficulty of the task. Excuses distance the person from the threat to their self-esteem and control. This is achieved by self-deception, minimising the self-focus so they do not need to 'engage in negative self-contemplation' (Snyder and Higgins, 1988, p. 29).

The three most difficult student reactions assessors reported were denial, anger and sadness. Denial, expressed as silence, indifference, flippancy or learnt helplessness, was the worst. It is an effective defence and attack. The absence of responsibility, projecting blame on to others or a lack of insight deprives staff of the opportunity to help, to encourage catharsis and change. Denial is a passive reaction which devalues 'the evaluations to the point where they no longer matter very much...distorts and degrades the assessment so it does not become a source of esteem' (Rowntree, 1987, p. 55). It may also be understood as the first stage of a reaction to a loss. Some respondents in Green's study (1991) described the act of failing and the ensuing feelings as almost an act of grieving and the process as one of bereavement.

Anger was the second most difficult reaction. It incorporated hostility, verbal aggression, bullying and threats to invoke legal action expressed by the student, their parents or the cohort. This seemed to be due to a dislike of conflict or confrontation, especially if unexpected: 'As a supervisor I expected to be respected, not dismissed. She was always questioning me, demanding reasons. She tried to bully me not to fail her.' Anger may be expressed by the students' parents or partner and the whole cohort. It can be a spur to action. A nursing student described being 'furious: angry at the system...angry for letting myself down...angry that there seemed to be nothing to gain from the experience' (Glover-Dell, 1990).

Sadness with a loss of self-esteem was the third most difficult student reaction reported by assessors. A manager noted 'if their self-worth is devastated, very distressed and unable to think of anything positive'. Other problematical responses were accusations of unfairness or misjudgement, surprise, niceness, manipulation and inconsistency.

Student reactions are more varied than just anger. The permutations of denial, anger and sadness may be understood as a natural reaction to a loss (Kubler-Ross, 1969) or redundancy (Hogg, 1991a). 'There is no panacea...understanding the emotions and knowing that thousands of others are going through a similar experience can help a great deal' (Hogg, 1991b, p. 12). This understanding is equally necessary for those who communicate the news, especially for the next phase of accepting the message. Staff describe wanting to provide a positive ending. Deferring this need, being able to contain and hold the student's reaction, is important. This process is analogous to analytic holding in that it demands the capacity 'to tolerate being genuinely in touch with what the other person is feeling, even to the extent of feeling those feelings oneself' (Casement, 1985, p. 153). A manager summarises this as 'failure is devastating but it is not the end of the world. It feels awful, an enormous blow. I encourage the student to talk this through.'

Acceptance

The penultimate phase of acceptance follows the emotional reaction. It involves reinforcing the reality of the situation. The fail grade is non-negotiable. It must be accepted before moving on to discuss resit strategies or different career options. Listening, allowing the students 'to talk and be honest about themselves', is important. This is the time when detailed feedback, examples, clarification and justification for the decision may be sought or heard. Acceptance involves reviewing the whole experience, all the losses and the gains from undertaking the course. The aim is to encourage the student to accept the rational reality at a cognitive and affective level; to minimise feelings of worthlessness by identifying achievements and learning gains. Acceptance may be considered as the springboard for the future.

Action

There are four main options which can be offered to a student who has failed a resit/final assessment. These are referral to the careers service, providing supportive references, ensuring they receive certificated recognition for the academic credits gained on the course, and information about appeals. They are practical strategies for moving forward. The immediate future encompasses how they will tell others, including family who may be disappointed, angry or blaming (see Chapter 4). The final interview can provide an opportunity to review and rehearse these options.

A future-orientated strategy is especially pertinent for students embarking upon a resit assignment or repeat work placement. This involves 'taking one step at a time, going to the right subject tutor for advice. Sometimes they are reluctant because they see themselves as failures and are not worth the time.' A work-practice organiser described seeing the student on their first day back in school to sort out the retake placement. These reflect causal attributions for the fail based upon inappropriate strategies, rather than low effort or ability. Help is instrumental not gratuitous (Graham, 1984), because methods for skills development are suggested (Clifford, 1986b) rather than responding with anger and criticism (Tollefson and Chen, 1988).

Considering future options also contributes to a positive ending. This is important for staff. In Ilott's (1993) study all reported a need to 'try to find something positive even if they are going on holiday. It should not finish without identifying the benefits – what they have gained and learned – from doing the course. If it does, the experience becomes destructive. It weighs on my conscience and I feel guilty' (p. 438). This quotation from an experienced manager illustrates the interdependence of a positive outcome for both staff and student. It also reflects the humanistic value of realistic optimism (Yerxa, 1983). There are two other, longer term factors which support a positive ending. These are recognising failure as part of life and learning, and reinforcing the purpose of summative assessment in professional training: 'I know what it is like to work with an incompetent colleague. I did not want be responsible for an unsafe therapist.' Both strategies combat the 'tendency to become immersed in visions of doom for a failing student' (Symanski, 1991, p. 21).

The final meeting or meetings are essential for closure. Leaving rituals recognise the losses which are inherent in separation, the consequence of termination of training. This section has described a range of strategies under the heading of the five As. These were: *anticipation* and planning; a clear unambiguous *announcement* of the result; expecting an emotive, including *angry*, response; encouraging *acceptance* because the fail is non-negotiable; and concluding with the *action* of forward planning.

Afterwards: coping with the aftermath

Fail scenarios do not end when the student leaves the training programme or work placement. The consequences can be enduring and diffuse. This assertion is illustrated by typical examples from work-based and academic assessors: 'It has been like a shadow hanging over me. It was five years ago and I still feel guilty. I felt awful. What had I ruined in just one afternoon? I was exhausted and put off having other students. All that effort, explaining to someone who was disinterested and not making any effort to learn. I did not gain anything. Why did I bother, particularly as there was not any back-up from the school. They did not stop her training' (supervisor). 'I had a sleepless night. I felt warmly towards the student but she could not cope with the academic work. It was a kindness for her. It was devastating for me' (manager). Both quotations emphasise the feelings (especially of guilt and sorrow) which can linger long after the student has gone.

This book concentrates upon the affective aspects of assessment decisions because feelings can sabotage judgements and undermine confidence. Disregarding feelings also perpetuates the myth about professionalism. This contributes to work stress, especially when professionals are required to be 'altruistic, dedicated, hard working and unselfish with regard for and devotion to the needs, interests and welfare of others' (Shah and Cooper, 1992, p. 26). This unselfishness is apparent in education. Although there has been considerable research into the effect of failure upon the individual and institution, little attention has been given to the staff perspective.

This section considers the repercussions of failing. These include a student appeal and dealing with complaints from angry parents. The confidence of examiners, especially inexperienced and work-based assessors, can be undermined with implications for other students. However, each fail provides learning opportunities. Some of the good practice revealed during Ilott's (1993) study are described so others may learn from this vicarious experience.

Complaints and appeals

The number and costs of complaints within higher education are increasing in the 1990s. This may be a consequence of consumerism as 'society is becoming more rights conscious and litigious' (Slapper, 1996). The trend is likely to continue with more students paying directly and indirectly for the privilege of higher education. An appeal is the final stage of the assessment process. In universities students are debarred from challenging staff judgement. The most usual criteria are procedural irregularities and undeclared extenuating circumstances. The right to and implications of an appeal have been recognised in other countries, particularly America where students may use the legal and educational systems (Darragh et al., 1986; Francis and Holmes, 1983; Pope, 1983; Streifer, 1987). The legal implications of marginal students are reviewed in several papers including Goclowski, 1985; Majorowicz, 1986; Poteet and Pollok, 1981 and Wood and Campbell, 1985. However, students are in a relatively powerless position. They have rights and responsibilities, as do staff. Familiarity with appeal procedures helps to avoid abuses and misuses.

Such knowledge and proper assessment systems can be protective, ensuring justice for all parties.

A student appeal is often feared by assessors. Those with experience describe the adversarial process as threatening and traumatic. A new manager commented on dealing with three appeals in the first year: 'They were an induction of fire. It was like going to court. It was very heavily weighted in favour of the student. I was a long and draining experience.' Another, with 25 years experience, described an appeal which was complicated by personal and health factors as the 'worst thing in my career'. An appeal can have an adverse effect upon other staff and the cohort. The threat of an appeal may even dissuade staff from giving a fail grade: 'The thought of an appeal frightened the supervisor. The student miraculously improved so much in the final week that she passed' (work-practice organiser). The adversarial format encourages alliances, conflict and anxiety. A manager outlined cohort responses: 'One appeal caused a lot of anguish amongst the students. In another case they thought the fail was fair. But there remains a legacy of anger amongst some students and work-place supervisors.'

An appeal undoubtedly increases the financial as well as the emotional costs of a fail. A manager described 'a water-tight case which took years to go through the formal appeal. It was very costly. The student lacked insight. It was difficult. In the end the questions have to be are we being fair and is the student safe?' Student rights need to be safeguarded but balanced with the purpose of assessment in professional training.

Parents and partners may complain about a fail grade. Grades are significant for parents too (Pollio et al., 1991). Complaints should be anticipated with female school leavers who are fulfilling parental career goals (Carpenito 1983, Meisenhelder 1982). Managers reported receiving visits and telephone calls from angry fathers, challenging the fairness and appropriateness of the result. For example: 'The father was difficult to reason with. He was very cross, believing his daughter had been victimised. He did not understand or accept what I was saying.' Opinion varied as to whether it was appropriate for staff to deal with parental reactions. This ranged from no, because 'the students are independent adults. I am not responsible to their parents' to yes, 'it is part of the grieving process for them. If the student wishes, then it is their right.' An agreed policy with clear boundaries and responsibilities for dealing with complaints from family members is useful in such situations. While staff cannot direct parental reactions, they can ensure fairness, concern and rigour of assessment practices. Documentation, which provides evidence about the application of these principles and due process, is an important safeguard.

Documenting due process

Making a record of all staff–student meetings is regarded as standard good practice. While the format may vary to comply with the guidelines set by the higher education institution, the record will usually summarise the purpose of the meeting, the agenda – the problems identified and action agreed – with the date for the next meeting. The student's file will usually contain details of meetings with personal tutors, academic staff and work-based supervisors. Students may be expected to maintain their own documents in the form of a learning log or reflective diary (Alsop and Ryan, 1996). The file should also contain an account or report of the work-placement supervision.

A signed, dated and contemporaneous record of the educational process is vital, especially when working with students at the margins of competence. The following examples illustrate the attention to the detail of these documents. A manager described making sure 'everything is well documented. All the formal and informal contacts which have a bearing on the failure. To ensure the outcomes of meetings are followed-up in writing with an acceptance proforma signed by the student.' A similar system was used by a work-practice organiser: 'I always provide a summary of the meeting and send a copy to all the relevant people. The student has the same information, they have formulated their learning contract, identified their strengths, weaknesses and objectives. This means the student has a voice and is not manipulated.'

Documentation may be considered as one of the examiners' best defences against complaints and self-recrimination. It demonstrates that justice has been done to the student, educational system and the public (Pope, 1983). Records are usually a main sources of evidence if the student invokes the grievance or appeal procedure. This is why they must be accurate, legible, complete, signed and dated. Documentary evidence also enhances objectivity by assisting the recall of critical incidents, behaviour, feedback, progress and action taken. They show the student has received due process. Students have a right to be assessed in a fair, equitable way. They are 'entitled to prior notice and an opportunity to be heard before s/he may be deprived of a protected right' (Wood and Campbell, 1985, p. 241). In America, records are required for the 'possibility where an educator may be sued for both failing, and not failing a student' (Goclowski, 1985, p. 104). This covers student appeals and educational malpractice. The latter is when 'failure to instruct properly (which includes passing a failing student and failing a passing student) may be a negligent act' (1985, p. 104). This recognises the assessor's dual responsibility – to the student and future service users – in professional training. Higher education institutions in the United Kingdom also need to be sensitive to this context of professional ethics and public service. Lenient appeal or progress systems which favour the student, allowing endless retakes to avoid complaints, do a disservice because they put future service users (whether patients, students or clients) at risk. They also further undermine staff confidence at a stressful time.

Sustaining confidence through support and learning

The support of colleagues, line managers and partners is a key mediating factor which helps assessors to survive a fail scenario. Support is a broad term which encompasses listening, understanding, giving a second opinion and advice. It involves gaining the agreement that the right decision has been made and will be implemented by all staff. Time is needed to discuss the decision, the reasons and how to avoid repetition of problems so it becomes a learning experience. Mutual awareness and monitoring such as 'saying "she was failing anyway". Noticing you are upset and need time' is valued. Support can vary depending upon a trusting relationship and whether the student is liked or disliked. Mixed support was described by a lecturer: 'Some give the impression "they all passed my assessment". They are blaming you as the teacher when you are vulnerable.' A supervisor related the support offered by a multidisciplinary health care team: 'There was a bit of leg pulling, such as "you must be an ogre", but they recognised she was not very good. They compared her unfavourably with other students.' This contrasts with the lack of support (from the employing agency, line managers, team and tutors) noted in Green's study (1991), where assessors' feelings were intensified by a sense of being isolated.

Sharing experiences with partners, relatives or friends is another source of support. Failing can be a work stress crossing the work–home boundary either directly or indirectly via 'headaches and a bad mood' (lecturer). The next two examples illustrate the strategies used by an experienced manager and supervisor dealing with her first fail: 'I tell a relative to lower my blood pressure. I take their wise advice. I am my own support because of my isolation. It is my judgement in the end. I need time to simmer and not to make instant judgements' (manager). 'At work I had to remain in control and professional. I could crack up at home. I live with colleagues so they knew what I was talking about. They were concerned because they could see my distress. They were relieved when the placement ended and I got back to normal' (supervisor).

The process of getting back to normal, regaining confidence in supervisory abilities, may require rest and recuperation. Work-based supervisors report 'not wanting to take a student ever again'. Their apprehension is encapsulated in this quotation: 'We were very careful and wary with the next student. We were frightened of doing the wrong thing. This is difficult to explain but we did not want to go through it all again. The placement organiser knew we only wanted a student who was going to pass.' It illustrates the enduring, ripple effect of a fail grade, particularly for undermining confidence.

A mixture of immediate and long-term support is likely to be appreciated by academic staff. The need for sensitivity (from colleagues and students) was explained by a lecturer who commented: 'I do not want it to be brought up again a year later. For example, by students saying "we must get it right because you failed so many last year" or to be reminded by staff. It might be my paranoia about things said in a flippant way. But they do not realise how it has affected you.' This quotation illustrates how empathy can be enhanced through listening. Talking is necessary for learning and closure: 'to get it off my chest. Not to unload it onto another person but to reflect on it. Then I can put the failure away – in a box on the shelf – so it can be taken down and used again' (lecturer).

Monitoring attrition, especially fail rates and reasons, is another way of learning from experience. Results are perceived to be a public, accountable way of assessing the quality of a course or institution. Internal and external monitoring mechanisms include statistical analysis of cohort results with historical and national comparisons which are presented in annual course reports or league tables. The validity and value of raw results as a performance indicator was considered in Chapter 1, especially the dilemmas associated with a causal theory of teaching, i.e. whether fails are accepted as part of the learning process and as an expression of standard setting, or as a reflection of poor quality teaching or facilities.

However, such debates should not obscure the value of debriefing for retrospective reflection and learning. This can involve reviewing particular cases or examining patterns which emerge from the cohort analysis. For example, a specific case can be analysed using a critical incident format to explore the thoughts, feelings and actions throughout the assessment cycle. The failure to fail in academic or work settings may be followed up to identify causes as a preventative tactic. A worst-case scenario is an effective, if unwelcome way of finding loopholes in procedures, support mechanisms and assessment regulations. Analysis of the cohort and patterns of results given by particular supervisors and work-place settings may reveal trends. These, with the 'normal' distribution curve, are useful to feed back to assessors for comparison. This good practice was described by a work-practice organiser: 'The supervisor only sees one fail. We view failure as a natural part of learning and the distribution curve. I monitor and feed back so the supervisors can see the results as a whole.' Such discussion also combats the taboos and negative stereotypes about failure, especially as they tend to be rare events.

Conclusion

This chapter has concentrated upon strategies for dealing with a fail. The intention was to demystify an infrequent, but onerous responsibility by placing it within the usual assessment cycle. The principles of alertness, eliciting, interpreting the evidence of competence and incompetence are pertinent for entry level practitioners and those undertaking continuing professional development. Honest, unambiguous feedback with action planning and documentation ensure the student's right to due process. They also demonstrate to the assessor that they have used effective strategies, done the best they can in the circumstances and fulfilled their role as a gatekeeper of professional standards.

Chapter 7
An executive summary with risks and recommendations for change

The final chapter takes the form of an executive summary. This is to provide the reader with a quick and easy overview of the whole book. As such it contains the key information, risks and strategies which are elaborated upon in earlier chapters.

Failure like other losses, is a forbidden topic. It has the status of a taboo. A 'terror of errors' pervades society. Failing provokes fear and dread. Reasons are ascribed and blame is apportioned. Failures, whether individual or institutional, are increasingly named and shamed as a way of provoking improvement whereas success is acclaimed. However, this strategy just perpetuates the stereotypes which provide the backdrop to failing in education and training. Yet failure is a natural part of life. It is one of the most powerful mechanisms and motivators for learning. Failure can be a positive life event for change. This is one of the themes which permeates the book, and it is boldly stated in this final chapter. Failing, like other losses, results in gains as well as losses. While the gains may not be immediately apparent, they usually become so with time. This is the message of the book. Although the context is circumscribed to education, particularly professional training, the message is germane. It reflects a saying of the author Bel Mooney 'Try, fail, try again. Fail better'(Scott, 1997).

Competence, at entry level and for continued practice, has been another theme (Chapter 2). Vocational courses prepare students to become skilled professionals working with the public in a range of capacities. All are characterised by trust. Service users – whether pupils, patients or clients – place their faith in the skill, knowledge and ethical behaviour of professionals. Any abuse of the power and privilege conferred by a professional relationship is heinous. This is why competence and conduct are of paramount concern. Professions have a duty to protect the public from unsafe, incompetent and unscrupulous colleagues (Chapter 2). The collective responsibility of professional and statutory bodies is vested in individual practitioners. This book is aimed at them, especially assessors in academic and practice settings.

Assigning a fail grade is an onerous responsibility for examiners. Judging that a student has not achieved the threshold standard of competence is a cognitively and emotionally exacting experience. Much attention has been given to the fears and feelings associated with fail scenarios (Chapter 4). This is because the affective aspects have been neglected (as has the whole topic of failure from the staff perspective) but, more importantly, because feelings influence thinking and behaviour. A sense of failure, guilt and anxiety can distort judgements and undermine confidence. Fears about reputations and student reactions mean marginal students are allowed to 'just pass'. Assessors can pay a high price for exercising their obligation to set minimum standards of professional practice. We hope appreciating the commonality of feelings will help examiners confront the taboo. This is important. The risks of not doing so are even higher, as evidenced by the examples of poor practice when practitioners do not achieve the threshold standards of quality and service which the public has a right to expect.

This is why the final chapter adopts a risk management approach to assigning a fail grade in vocational courses. Risk management is the process of identifying, analysing, controlling and evaluating to minimise risks, in order to protect all parties concerned (Roy, 1996). The main benefits are long term, with the prevention of 'horror stories' about the abuse of vulnerable service users. This perspective is needed in a free market with a utilitarian climate because it counters the immediate pressure of performance indicators, league tables or financial viability. It is the rationale for making pass–fail decisions.

Risk management strategies

Risk management strategies for individual and institutions are presented in this executive summary so as to reflect the complex causality. There are many reasons why failing is so difficult. These encompass individual, institutional and external factors (Chapter 3). Each fail is unique with its own set of meanings, circumstances and consequences. Understanding the reasons and risks is the starting point for action. The time is also right due to the increasing demands for accountability in higher and vocational education. All parties need to be assured of good judgements, based upon best assessment practices (Chapters 5 and 6). This is to protect the rights and responsibilities of students and staff, the good name of the professions, but ultimately to safeguard the public.

Risks and strategies for individuals

Risk: Failure taboo sabotages good judgements.
Strategy: Challenge negative stereotypes and accept failing as part of life and learning.

It is imperative to understand the meaning of the fail grade. It is a unidimensional symbol with multidimensional meanings (Chapter 1). There is an assumption that a fail is unwelcome and unwanted. It may be neither. Only the student knows the personal meaning – the relevance, value and importance of the grade. The social meaning also needs to be challenged. Failure can be condemned by others. This reflects a terror of errors rather than viewing failure as a learning experience and opportunity. Much learning occurs by trial and error, learning by and from mistakes. Failing can be a powerful motivator which stimulates adaptation and change. Understanding the learning potential counters the trait meaning. Failure to achieve the required standard on one task does not mean the person is a failure. Failure on one task does not automatically transfer to all other tasks. These fixed and self-fulfilling assumptions need to be contradicted. Understanding the multiple and positive meanings is the starting point for allaying the fears and fallacies associated with the taboos.

Risk: Feelings interfere with thinking and behaviour.
Strategy: Understand the common pattern of feelings and prepare for student responses.

Assigning a fail grade is a work stress which can provoke anxiety and distress (Chapter 4). These feelings, supported by guilt, can impair rational decision making and lead to avoidance of the word and deed. Yet passing a failing student is the equivalent of educational malpractice. Understanding the common pattern of feelings as a natural, rather than overwhelming or abnormal, reaction offers assurance. This is matched by predicting student responses to the news. While distress is expected, anger and relief are common, depending upon the personal meaning of the loss (Chapter 6). Perhaps the most important feeling is that of pride from completing a difficult task well, fulfilling a professional obligation to maintain standards of practice. Surely, this is preferable to the guilt and regret associated with the failure to fail.

Risk: Disrespect for minimum, threshold standards of competence.
Strategy: Apply sound assessment principles.

The assessment of competence to practice is a complex, controversial topic. However the converse – incompetence – is easier to define and identify. There seems to be an unspoken, interdisciplinary consensus about what constitutes a fail grade (Chapter 2). Conduct – professional, ethical behaviour not profession-specific knowledge or skills – is given priority. All contribute to an explicit reference level against which evidence is elicited, interpreted and acted upon during the assessment cycle. Assessors in academic or work settings have a duty to combine objective and subjective evidence about both competence and incompetence. Evidence needs to be obtained from as valid, reliable methods as is possible, with third parties giving an independent, second opinion. All the documented evidence is then judged on the 'balance of probabilities' or 'beyond reasonable doubt' with the latter, stronger burden of proof and certainty being recommended for a final, summative assessment. Applying these best principles protects staff from self and other's accusations of wrong or unfair decision making (Chapters 5 and 6).

Risk: Conflict in values and subjectivity can lead to collusion.
Strategy: Sensitivity to high risk factors.

Alertness to factors which add to the difficulty of awarding a fail grade may be viewed as a preventative strategy (Chapter 3). The conflict in values and roles seems to be a fundamental factor. Professionals who espouse humanistic values offer unconditional positive regard, encourage success and reward effort. These values underpin work with service users and students to such an extent that there is an antipathy towards being judgmental and judging threshold standards. Blurring the boundaries between educator and practitioner can tip the balance between roles and responsibilities. Other factors which make failing more difficult include the assessor's inexperience, their susceptibility to identification with the student and lack of support from the educational programme. Some students are particularly hard to fail. These include finalist students, those who are liked, hard working and committed to the career. However, these subjective factors must be weighed against objective evidence of the attainment of minimum standards of safety and competency.

Risk and strategy for educational programmes – institutions

Risk: Reputation for low standards.
Strategy: Counter the causal theory of teaching.

Reputations are the 'brand names' of educational institutions. Poor reputations are easy to gain but difficult to lose. Standards, whether threshold or for excellence, are a corporate responsibility but set through individual assessors. The causal theory of teaching connects individuals and institutions (Chapter 3). This theory assumes a direct relationship between teaching and learning with teachers accountable for success and failure. It is simplistic, denying socio-economic factors or learning as an active, equal partnership. The causal theory blames teachers when students fail (even though a small number may be considered part of a so-called normal distribution curve). This is transferred to institutions when outputs rather than longer term outcomes are quality indicators on league tables. The causal theory influences perceptions, particularly whether fails represent poor teaching or testify to minimum standards. There can be pressure to moderate grades upwards to create a good impression and position on result league tables. It is important to strike a balance for an absence of fails is as suspect as grade inflation.

Risk: Institutional inertia about assessment regulations and quality assurance.

Strategy: Promote good assessment practices.

Effective, efficient assessment methods supported by appropriate regulations and procedures are key components of quality education (Chapter 5). There will always be a trade-off between ideal assessment principles and their application in the 'real world' of academic and practice settings. Yet the ideal should be striven for. Action based upon sound evidence is supportive, especially at student appeals (Chapter 6). Preparing educators for their role as assessors is important. Specific preparation about fail scenarios offers vicarious experience, gives permission to use the full range of marks, reinforces good educational practices, but most importantly confers confidence.

Open, transparent assessment regulations which encompass worst-case scenarios and use the word fail are also essential. Regulations need to accommodate the special concerns of vocational courses about professional suitability and mental health, for example. Such courses have a duty to give priority to public protection rather than student rights. A review of institutional mechanisms which deny failure (such as the ritual of pass lists) and the losses associated with attrition would also offer a more humane and rational approach to failure.

Risk: Widening the theory–practice gap.

Strategy: Provide an outreach support network for work-based assessors.

The goal of academic and work-based educators is to produce a competent professional who is fit for purpose, practice and award (Chapter 2). It is an important shared goal. This provides a strong bond between those responsible for different aspects of pre- and post-registration training programmes. Although staff in each setting are subject to conflicting priorities, from providing the service to meeting research assessment exercise targets, ensuring competence to practise is an enduring obligation. It can be promoted through joint training and working. This requires a properly resourced and valued outreach network of work-practice organisers. Their role as independent and impartial advisers is equivalent to that of external examiners and deserves a similar status.

Risks from and strategies for dealing with wider, external pressures

Risk: Positive action for international students.

Strategy: Equal opportunities and fair reference levels.

Students from other countries who study in the United Kingdom contribute a rich cultural mix. They are a ready source of income at a time of under-funding for home entrants. In the academic year 1996/97 international students comprised 12 per cent (n=198,400) of the population at UK higher education colleges and universities. Most (22.3 per cent) are postgraduate students with 8.2 per cent on first degree programmes. International students obtain a higher percentage of first class honours (8.1 per cent) compared with all entrants (6.9 per cent). A much higher percentage are awarded third class honours, almost twice the proportion of all first degree students (Nye, 1997). Third class and pass degrees are generally considered 'not satisfactory' (Charter, 1997), i.e. to represent a failure to fail. These statistics can be seen to indicate double standards which brings UK higher education into disrepute for both exploitation and grade inflation (Chapter 6).

Clear, explicit reference levels which contain the learning outcomes or course specifications (or any other synonymous term) are essential for equal opportunities.

They can counter both discrimination and leniency. This is important if different cultural reactions to failure are taken into account. The career of post-registration students in their home countries may be tainted for many years. A prime example is overseas doctors who do not gain membership of a Medical Royal College during their period of residence in the UK. Undergraduates on professional training courses may carry the extra responsibility of self or government sponsorship to develop services on their return. Although they may not attain threshold standards for the UK, their performance may be judged acceptable for a developing country and service. The dilemma is that a pass grade permits registration to practise anywhere (in the UK and eligibility to apply to other countries such as the USA, Canada, Australia and New Zealand) and not just their country of origin. All these factors are extra, external pressures which can impinge upon assessors' judgements.

Risk: Professional protectionism.
Strategy: Strengthen regulation of entry level and continued competence.

Ensuring competence to practise is the primary duty of statutory and professional bodies (Chapter 2). It is a career-long obligation which extends from entry level competence to continued professional development. Accountability is exercised via approval of training courses and disciplinary hearings which can result in being 'struck off' the register of practitioners. Such judgements are devolved to individual practitioners. Regulation requires more than effective systems with sensitive, swift responses to complaints. Peers must muster the courage to enforce standards of competency at pre- and post-qualifying levels. If not, trust is lost and integrity is jeopardised as a self-serving profession is seen to protect its monopoly rather than the public. Legal responsibility is vested in individuals. Professional self-regulation is a privilege which can be abused, denied or accepted. This book promotes the latter – action – as the only acceptable strategy.

Conclusion

The elusive concept of professionalism proves to be both the key criterion for competence and the main mediating factor for confronting failure as an essential but difficult aspect of an assessors' role and responsibilities. Debates about definitions of a profession or semi-profession and about which occupation deserves such status are esoteric. There is a common 'bottom line' regardless of setting, service provided or client group. This is the prevention of the abuse of power, whether by staff unjustly failing students, practitioners exploiting vulnerable service users or students threatening assessors.

We hope this book will help reduce the failure to fail by helping assessors make well informed judgements for the right reasons. Examiners who do this are not ogres (a word much used in the quotations), cruel or uncaring, for failing can be 'a higher form of caring, responsibility and accountability to the student, the client and the profession' (Carpenito, 1983).

Appendix 1
Disciplinary Committee of the Occupational Therapists Board Statement of Infamous Conduct

Introduction

This Statement of Conduct applies to all registered occupational therapists

1. The Statement which follows is required by the Professions Supplementary to Medicine Act 1960. It provides for every registered occupational therapist an indication of the kind of conduct which the Committee considers to be 'infamous in a professional respect'. This means misconduct which is serious enough to bring the profession into disrepute and consequently render the person concerned unfit to be registered.

Providing a good standard of practice and care

2. Registrants must discharge their duties and responsibilities in a professional, ethical and moral manner. Patients and clients are entitled to receive good and safe standards of practice and care. The Statement is intended to protect the patient/client from unprofessional and unethical behaviour, ensuring such standards are maintained by registrants. These standards are required primarily for the protection of the public rather than the benefit of the profession. The Statement therefore imposes additional responsibilities on registrants to those required of the ordinary citizens

Interpreting the Statement

3. Registrants must be familiar with the Statement and ensure that they apply it in their practice as occupational therapists. The Committee will use the Statement when it considers cases where a registrant has been

accused of infamous conduct. When considering such cases in the light of the Statement, the Committee will, when appropriate, take account of the 'Code of Ethics and Professional Conduct for Occupational Therapists' of the College of Occupational Therapists, with particular reference to Sections 5.1 on clinical competence and 5.2 on delegation. The Committee expects that Registrants will be familiar with and apply the College's Code in their practice as occupational therapists. They must also take all reasonable steps to ensure that they can communicate properly and effectively with their patients/clients.

It is the registrant's prime duty in all circumstances to have proper regard to the patient's/client's welfare

4. While the Statement contains a number of specific instances, it is impossible to compile a complete list of conduct which may at some time be regarded by the Committee as infamous. The Committee may judge a person to be guilty of infamous conduct even though the matter in question is not explicitly mentioned in the Statement. It therefore emphasises that whatever is contained in the Statement and the College's Code, every case referred to it will be considered on its own merits and in the light of the registrants' duty to have proper regard to the welfare of a patient so that the health or safety of the patient is not endangered.*

Criminal offences

5. The Committee may, if it thinks fit, remove from the register the name of a person who has been convicted by any Court in the United Kingdom of a criminal offence which the Committee decides renders him or her unfit to be registered. It may also do so where it is satisfied that the name of such a person has been fraudulently registered.

Enquiries

6. If there is uncertainty or dispute as to the interpretation or application of the Statement, enquiries should be referred, in the first instance to the Registrar at Park House, 184 Kennington Park Road, London SE11 4BU.

---

* It would not be proper for the Committee to be involved in the merits of any industrial dispute concerning registrants and their employers, and the participation by registrants in industrial action would not be regarded as within the Statement of Conduct which is concerned only with infamous conduct in a professional respect. The Disciplinary Committee will consider any allegation referred to it, irrespective of whether or not the conduct complained of has arisen in the course of industrial action or in any other circumstances.

Statement

With these considerations in mind, the Committee wishes to bring to the notice of all registered occupational therapists in whatever location or context, that in its view failure to observe the requirements set out below would be the kind of conduct which it considers to be infamous conduct in a professional respect.

a) No occupational therapist should by any act or omission do anything or cause anything to be done which in the opinion of the Committee may either endanger or affect adversely in a substantial way the health or safety of a patient/client or patients/clients.**

b) Advertising by registered occupational therapists in respect of professional activities shall be accurate and restrained. Advertisements, whether written or audio-visual, should not be false, fraudulent, misleading, deceptive, self-laudatory, unfair or sensational. Explicit claims should not be made in respect of superiority of personal skills, equipment or facilities. Professional signs should be dignified and professionally restrained.

c) (Subject to any subsequent variations which may be made after the Home Secretary has issued the eventual Order under the Data Protection Act based on the DHSS draft guidelines contained in the 'Code of Confidentiality of Personal Health Data') a registered occupational therapist should in the course of professional work seek, keep or store and disclose health information about a patient/client solely for the purpose of that patient's/client's continuing care. It is considered that an occupational therapist who has carefully followed the 'Code of Confidentiality of Personal Health Data', while practising in the United Kingdom, for example in relation to disclosure of information, will not be in breach of this requirement.

d) No registered occupational therapist should in any way exploit or abuse the relationship between occupational therapist and patient/client.

e) A registered occupational therapist may have a professional relationship with a carer as well as patient/client. In these circumstances the requirements of a), c) and d) above will extend to the relationship with the carer.

**For registrants' guidance, the Committee specifies one example of where an 'omission' could be considered to be infamous conduct within the terms of this paragraph. This would be failure to communicate, in situations other than those covered by identified proper and specific local arrangements, with a relevant medical practitioner in the management of a patient/client or patients/clients. A 'patient' or 'client' is an individual for whom the therapist has a direct clinical responsibility. In this context, the supervising occupational therapist has the overall clinical responsibility for the treatment of the patients/clients undertaken by a student. June 1996.

Glossary

Similar terms may describe different features of the educational process in different professions. In this book certain educational terms have been used consistently with specific meanings. This glossary defines and explains how they are used.

Assessors – examiners

The terms 'examiner' and 'assessor' have overlapping meanings in a variety of contexts. Both involve staff in appraising student performance against a benchmark (whether implicit or explicit) and then making a value judgement which is expressed as a symbol such as grade, percentage mark, degree classification or phrase.

Academic assessor/examiner: the lecturer responsible for judging the quality of students' work undertaken in academic settings. This term is used to distinguish and differentiate between work-based assessors who judge students in practice settings.

Manager: the generic term covering course leaders, heads of schools, programme directors or other equivalent managerial roles in higher education. They are senior academics with managerial responsibility and accountability for a specific educational programme. In some professional programmes it is the manager who would usually inform students of the outcome of their assessment as ratified by the examination board. This may be a resit assessment, repeating a work-based placement or withdrawal from the programme. Such managers may also coordinate responses to a student appeal and deal with complaints from the student's parents and partner.

Work-based assessor: a member of staff employed by an agency providing a service (for example, a hospital, school or social services department) who judges the quality of students' performances in the practice setting.

Moderation and validation

Internal moderation: occurs when comparisons are made between the assessment standards being applied by different individuals. Often this can involve some independent, cross marking of students' work. The results can be compared for similarities and differences in the way pieces of work are being judged. This can involve a process of negotiation over how to resolve any differences. Internal moderation can relate to individual pieces of work or the work of an entire cohort of students.

External moderation/examining: a similar process often undertaken by external examiners appointed by the higher education institution. External examiners are senior members of staff from other higher education institutions. Their role is twofold: to ensure fairness to the student within the course regulations as individuals and, second, in relation to their peers to ensure comparable standards across the higher education sector.

Validation: the formal procedure for approving a programme of study. The quality of the curriculum, facilities and staff are reviewed through peer review with internal and external colleagues. Some professional programmes may even be required to undergo tripartite validation to satisfy the academic requirements of the higher education institution, the requirements of the professional and statutory bodies and employers' expectations of current competent performance in the workplace.

Work-based settings, processes and supervisors

Work-based placement: many professional education programmes contain a considerable period of work-based learning. This entails learning while doing a job with varying degrees of supervision from work-based supervisors and others who may visit the students while on placement.

The professional and statutory bodies may set a minimum number of hours for work-based practice. For example, the standards set for education programmes by the World Federation of Occupational Therapists (WFOT) require a minimum of 1,000 hours of work experience under the supervision of an occupational therapist in different settings which provide services to individuals with different problems. This is equivalent to one-third of a pre-registration three-year degree course in the United Kingdom. There is an even higher proportion for students preparing to become school teachers on the one-year Post Graduate Certificate of Education (PGCE). The school-based element constitutes 22 weeks of a 36-week course.

The General Medical Council (GMC) has a criteria of 5,500 hours medical training which includes a year as a Pre-registration House Officer. The pre-registration year is the sixth and final year of basic medical education. Universities are responsible for ensuring the posts (which may comprise four months in medicine, surgery and general practice) provide good experience, supervision and training. The purpose of general clinical training is

> to enable PRHOs to put into practise the key skills that they have learned and apply knowledge gained during undergraduate medical education
> to enable PRHOs to demonstrate that on completing general clinical training, they are ready to accept with confidence the duties and responsibilities of a fully registered doctor and to begin training for specialist medical practice. (GMC, 1997)

Work-based practice within professional education is usually assessed. The result may contribute to the degree classification or be a pass–fail grade. Assessment may be the sole responsibility of the work-based supervisor or shared with an academic staff member. For example, satisfactory completion of the PRHO year is a pre-requisite for eligibility for full registration with the General Medical Council. A Certificate of Satisfactory Service is issued at the end of each four- or six-month post by the supervising consultant. The PRHO is 'signed up' through a Certificate of Experience on satisfactory completion of the year.

Supervisor/mentor/work-placement trainer: the practitioner responsible for supervising students during the work-based placement. In the apprenticeship, model supervisors are the experts, the role models to be imitated. Supervisors are often expected to combine pastoral, teaching and assessment roles. Thus they can provide support, enable learning and evaluate attainment of the learning outcomes for the student's stage of training. This can be achieved through graded exposure to real work through the stages of observation, directed practice to be supervised and finally, independent practice as preparation for and to simulate entry level responsibilities. In this way students experience practical preparation designed to complement the theoretical components of the programme.

Work-based supervisors offer more than support for students as they develop highly specific, professional skills. Practitioners contribute to professional socialisation. The situation is 'not merely a context for acquiring craft skills; it also represents fundamental initiation rites through which student teachers acquire implicit professional norms governing acceptable thought and behaviour expected of teachers' (Holligan, 1997). This raises questions about the appropriateness of such norms, and about professional practices which can remain static if too much reliance is placed upon an apprenticeship approach to initial preparation.

Training the next generation is a professional obligation which is often not compensated by payment or a reduction in the demands of their primary role as practitioners. There is an increasing number of 'training the trainers' courses to enhance the educational knowledge and skills of supervisors.

Work-practice organisers: the members of academic staff responsible for selecting, coordinating and monitoring work-based placements. While all lecturers may undertake review and assessment visits to students in work settings there is usually one person with overall responsibility for the practice component of the curriculum. Their role is to develop partnership relationships to ensure sufficient, suitable work placements. This includes accrediting or judging the quality of placements, training and supporting supervisors and auditing the performance of the cohort in work-based settings.

Professional courses

Profession: a broad definition has been adopted in this book. Professions encompass occupations which offer a service, often in the public rather than private sector. Members of a profession are contacted directly or indirectly by service users (another generic term to encompass patients, clients or students for example) because of their special knowledge or skill. Service users expect professionals to demonstrate a certain competence and ethical conduct. Professions and professionals possess a particular body of knowledge, are autonomous but also accountable for offering an effective and efficient service, and may be motivated by altruism rather than the profit.

Vocational courses: in this book this category relates to aspects of the initial training of professionals. Vocational courses prepare students for entry level competence – the knowledge, skills and attitude expected from newly qualified practitioners. There is also a requirement, whether mandatory or voluntary, to maintain and extend competence throughout a professional career. This is referred to as continued competence or continued professional development.

National Occupational Standards: are precise descriptions of what is required of an individual at work. They are based on the outcomes of successful performance and are benchmarks. They are developed under the auspices of a lead body or occupational standards council which comprise employer representatives. National occupational standards must meet certain criteria relating to their content, structure and processes used for their development, such as functional analysis. They form the basis – or units – of National Vocational Qualifications.

National Vocational Qualifications: have been developed during the last decade to improve the capability and competitiveness of the UK workforce. They are intended to have parity of esteem with academic qualifications. Vocational qualifications require the progressive specification of key purpose and roles into clearly identifiable outcomes for the occupational sector.

References

Adshead D, Allen W, Bahrami J, Belton A, Heywood P, Jenkinson S, Lewis A, Stanley I, Varnavides C. (1984) Helping those who fail the MRCGP examination. Medical Teacher 6, 3: 101–5.

Alexander H (1996) Physiotherapy student clinical education: the influence of subjective judgements on observational assessment. Assessment and Evaluation in Higher Education 21, 4: 357–65.

Allsop J, Mulcahy L (1996) Regulating Medical Work: Formal and Informal Controls. Buckingham: Open University Press.

Alsop A, Ryan S (1996) Making the Most of Fieldwork Education: A Practical Approach. London: Chapman & Hall.

Alsop AE (1991) Five Schools Project: Clinical Practice Curriculum Development. Oxford: Dorset House School of Occupational Therapy.

Atkins MJ, Beattie J, Dockrell WB (1993) Assessment Issues in Higher Education. Sheffield: Employment Department Group.

Baldwin PJ, Newton RW, Buckley G, Roberts MA, Dodd M (1997) Senior House Officers in medicine: postal survey of training and work experience. British Medical Journal 314:740–3.

Barker J (1990) A model of clinical evaluation. Australian Journal of Occupational Therapy 37, 4: 198–203.

Barnett R (1994) The Limits of Competence: Knowledge, Higher Education and Society. Buckingham: The Society for Research into Higher Education and Open University Press.

Barnitt RE (1996) An Investigation of Ethical Dilemmas in Occupational Therapy and Physiotherapy: Issues of Methodology and Practice. Unpublished PhD thesis, University of London.

Bastos MW, Fletcher C (1995) Exploring the individual's perception of sources and credibility of feedback in the work environment. International Journal of Selection and Assessment 3, 1: 29-40.

Baty P (1997) A-level English passes off the mark. The Times Higher Education Supplement, 10 January: 1.

Berrie T (1998) Personal Communication. Assistant Registrar. Council for the Professions Supplementary to Medicine.

Black P, Wiliam D (1998) Assessment and classroom learning. Assessment in Education 5, 1: 7–74.

Bligh D (1994) Assessing Professional People by OSPRE. Exeter: Police Review Publishing Co Ltd and Lyndean Associates.

Bligh D, Jaques D, Warren-Piper D (1981) Seven Decisions when Teaching Students. Devon: Exeter University Teaching Services.

Blomquist KB (1985) Evaluation of students: intuition is important. Nurse Educator 10 8: 8–11.

Boekaerts M (1991) Subjective competence appraisals and self-assessment. Learning and Instruction 1: 1–17.

Boydell D (1986) Issues in teaching practice supervision research: a review of the literature. Teaching and Teacher Education 2, 2: 115–25.

Bradley J (1990) Assessing the Clinical Progress of Student Nurses. Unpublished MPhil dissertation, University of Nottingham.

Bradshaw MJ, Lowenstein L (1990) Perspectives on academic dishonesty. Nurse Educator 15, 5: 10–15.

Brandon J, Davies M (1979) The limits of competence in social work: the assessment of marginal students in social work education. British Journal of Social Work 9, 3: 295–347.

Brinko KT (1993) The practice of giving feedback to improve teaching. Journal of Higher Education 64, 5: 574–93.

Broadfoot P (1994) Editorial. Assessment in Education 1, 1: 3–9.

Brozenec S, Marshall JR, Thomas C, Walsh M, (1987) Evaluating borderline students. Journal of Nursing Education 26, 1: 42–44.

Buckman R, Kason Y (1992) How to Break Bad News: A Guide for Health-care Professionals. London: Papermac.

Burrows E (1989) Clinical practice: an approach to the assessment of clinical competencies. British Journal of Occupational Therapy 52, 6: 222–6.

Calman K (1996) Departmental News from the Chief Medical Officer. Health Trends 28, 1: 1–2

Cameron R, Wilson S (1993) The practicum: student-teacher perceptions of teacher supervision styles. South Pacific Journal of Teacher Education 21, 2: 155–67.

Caney D (1983) Competence – can it be assessed? Physiotherapy 69, 8: 302–4.

Carlisle D (1996) Managed misdemeanours. Health Service Journal, 17 October: 13–14.

Carpenito LJ (1983) The failing or unsatisfactory student. Nurse Educator 8, 4: 32–3.

Casement P (1985) On Learning from the Patient. London: Tavistock Publications.

Charter D (1996) Inspectors say poor marking is harming vocational courses. The Times, 14 June: 6.

Charter D (1997) Standards are all a question of degree. The Times, 18 July: 37.

Chesser A, Brett M (1989) Clinical teaching in context: a factor analysis of student ratings. Research in Medical Education. Proceedings of the 28th Annual Conference Association of American Medical Colleges: 49–54.

Claxton G (1984) Live and Learn. An Introduction to the Psychology of Growth and Change in Everyday Life. London: Harper and Row.

Clifford MM (1986a) The comparative effects of strategy and effort attributions. British Journal of Educational Psychology 56: 75–83.

Clifford MM (1986b) The effect of ability, strategy and effort attributions for educational, business and athletic failure. British Journal of Educational Psychology 56: 167–79.

Clift PS (1990) School Self Evaluation. In Fitz-Gibbon CT (Ed.) Performance Indicators. BERA Dialogues No. 2. Clevedon: Multilingual Matters Ltd.

Clothier C, Macdonald CA, Shaw DA (1994) The Allitt Inquiry. London: HMSO.

Coates VE, Chambers M (1992) Evaluation of tools to assess clinical competence. Nurse Education Today 12: 122–9.

Cogger W (1994) Professional standards in 1994 – and beyond. Yorkshire Medicine. Autumn: 6.

Cohen GS, Blumberg P (1991) Investigating whether teachers should be given assessments of students made by previous teachers. Academic Medicine 66, 5: 288–9.

Cohn ES, Frum DC (1988) Fieldwork supervision: more education is warranted. American Journal of Occupational Therapy 42, 5: 325–7.

Collins JP, White GR (1993) Selection of Auckland medical students over 25 years: a time for change? Medical Education 27: 321–7.

Cornwell T (1997) Disclosure plea on PhDs. Times Higher Education Supplement, 25 April: 8.

Council for National Academic Awards (1992) Academic Quality in Higher Education: A Guide to Good Practice in Framing Regulations. London: CNAA.

Council for Professions Supplementary to Medicine (1979) The Next Decade. London: CPSM.

Crocker LM, Muthard JE, Slaymaker JE, Samson L (1975) A performance rating scale for evaluating clinical competence of occupational therapy students. American Journal of Occupational Therapy 29, 2: 81–6.

Croen LG, Reichgott M, Spencer RK (1991) A performance-based method for early identification of medical students at risk of developing academic problems. Academic Medicine 66, 8: 486–8.

Darragh R, Jacobson G, Sloan B, Sandquist G (1986) Unsafe student practice: policy and procedures. Nursing Outlook 34, 4: 176–8.

Davenhall E (1985) The assessment of practical skills in nursing students. Unpublished MPhil dissertation, Sheffield City Polytechnic.

Davies P, Van der Gaag A (1992) The professional competence of speech therapists. Part 1: Introduction and methodology. Clinical Rehabilitation 6: 209–14.

Dell MS, Valine WJ (1990) Explaining differences in NCLEX–RN scores with certain cognitive and non–cognitive factors for new baccalaureate nurse graduates. Journal of Nursing Education 29, 4: 158–62.

Department for Education and Employment (1996) Higher Level Vocational Qualifications: A Government Position Paper. Sheffield: DfEE.

Donaldson LJ (1994) Doctors with problems in an NHS workforce. British Medical Journal 308: 1277–82.

Dopson L (1987) Final curtains? Nursing Times, 4 February: 18–19.

Duffy B. (1987) Clinical conduct. Senior Nurse 6, 2: 13–14.

Eble KE (1976) Teaching and Learning in Higher Education. London: Penguin Books.

Editorial (1993) Patients come first. The Times, 19 May: 17.

Eisenhart M, Behm L, Romagnano L (1990) Learning to teach: developing expertise or rite of passage. Journal of Education for Teaching 17, 1: 51–71.

Eraut M (1994) Developing Professional Knowledge and Competence. London: Falmer Press.

Eraut M, Steadman S, Trill J, Parkes J. (1996) The Assessment of NVQs. Research Report No. 4. Brighton: University of Sussex Institute of Education.

Eraut MR, Cole G (1993) Assessing Competence in the Professions. Research and Development Series No. 14. Sheffield: Employment Department.

Ericson DP, Ellett FS (1987) Teacher accountability and the causal theory of teaching. Educational Theory 32, 3: 277–93.

Fenn P, Hermans D, Dingwall R (1994) Estimating the cost of compensating victims of medical negligence. British Medical Journal 309: 389–91.

Fine SA (1988) Functional Job Analysis. Chapter 9.2 in The Job Analysis Handbook for Business Industry and Government. New York: John Wiley & Sons.

Ford J, Jones A (1987) Student Supervision. Houndmills: Macmillan Education Ltd.

Ford R (1994) Child abuser Beck dies in prison after heart attack. The Times, 2 June: 5.

Francis AS, Holmes SE (1983) Criterion referenced standard setting in certification and licensure: defining the minimally competent candidate. Paper presented at the American Psychological Association.

Fraser D, Murphy RJL, Worth-Butler M (1997) An Outcome Evaluation of the Effectiveness of Pre-Registration Midwifery Programmes of Education. London: English National Board for Nursing, Midwifery and Health Visitors Research Report.

Freidson E (1994) Professionalism Reborn: Theory Philosophy and Policy. Cambridge: Polity Press.

Friedman M, Mennin SP (1991) Rethinking critical issues in performance assessment. Academic Medicine 66, 7: 390–5.

Gealy N, Johnson C, Miller C, Mitchell L (1990) Designing Assessment Systems for National Certification. In Fennel E. (Ed.) (1991) Development of Assessable Standards for National Certification. Sheffield: Employment Department Group.

Geary, A (1988) Written judgements in school: a personal perspective. Early Child Development and Care 34: 241–65.

General Medical Council (1995) Good Medical Practice. London: GMC).

General Medical Council (1997) The New Doctor. London: GMC.

Gibbs G (1992) Teaching More Students: 4. Assessing More Students. London: The Polytechnics and Colleges Funding Council.

Gilfoyle E (1984) Eleanor Clarke Slagle Lectureship 1984: Transformation of a profession. American Journal of Occupational Therapy 38: 575–84.

Gipps CV (1994) Beyond Testing: Towards a Theory of Educational Assessment. London: Falmer Press.

Gipps CV, Murphy P (1994) A Fair Test? Assessment Achievement and Equity. Buckingham: Open University Press.

Gleason JJ (1984) UGAP: help for failing students. Academic Therapy 20, 2: 217–20.

Glover-Dell M (1990) A failed nurse. Nursing Standard 5, 10: 54.

Goclowksi J (1985) Legal implications of academic dismissal and educational malpractice for nursing faculty. Journal of Nursing Education 24, 3: 104–8.

Goldenberg D, Waddall J (1990) Occupational stress and coping strategies among female baccalaureate nursing faculty. Journal of Advanced Nursing 15: 531–43.

Gonczi A (1994) Competency based assessment in the professions in Australia. Assessment in Higher Education 1, 1: 27–44.

Graham S (1984) Teacher feeling and student thoughts: an attributional approach to affect in the classroom. The Elementary School Journal 85, 1: 91–104.

Green C (1991) Identification of the responsibilities and perceptions of the training task held by workforce supervisors of those training within the caring professions. Project 551 prepared for the Further Education Unit, Anglia Polytechnic.

Gupta GC (1991) Student attrition: a challenge for allied health education programs. JAMA, August, 21: 963–7.

Gutman SA, McCreedy P, Heisler P (1998) Student level II fieldwork failure: strategies for intervention. American Journal of Occupational Therapy 52, 2: 143–9.

Hager P, Gonczi A (1996) What is competence? Medical Teacher 18, 1: 15–18.

Harvey L, Moon S, Geall V, Bower R (1997) Graduates' Work: Organisational Change and Students' Attributes. Birmingham: Centre for Research into Quality, University of Central England.

Harvey TJ, Vaughan J (1990) Student nurse attitudes towards different teaching/learning methods. Nurse Education Today 10: 181–5.

Hausman CI, Weiss JC, Lawrence JS, Zelenznik C (1990) Confidence weighted answer techniques in a group of paediatric residents. Medical Teacher 12, 2: 163–8.

Henkin Y, Friedman M, Bouskila D, Kushnir D, Glick S (1990) The use of patients as student evaluators. Medical Teacher 12, 2/4: 279–88

Heywood J (1989) Assessment in Higher Education. Chichester: John Wiley & Sons.

Heywood L, Gonczi A, Hager P (1992) A guide to development of competency standards for professions. National Office of Overseas Skills Recognition Research Paper No. 7. Canberra: Australian Government Publishing Service.

Higher Education Quality Council (1994) External Examining in Focus. London: HEQC.

Higher Education Quality Council (1995) Graduate Standards Programme. Interim Report Executive Summary. London: HEQC.

Higher Education Quality Council (1997) Assessment in Higher Education and the Role of 'Graduateness'. London: HEQC.

Higher Education Quality Council/National Health Service Executive (1996) Improving the Effectiveness of Quality Assurance Systems in Non-Medical Health Care Education and Training. London: HEQC.

Hodson P. (1993) Tough Interviews. Video. Melrose Film Productions, 16 Bromwells Road, London SW4 0BL.

Hogg C (1991a) Coping with the first 24 hours. The Times, 14 November.

Hogg C (1991b) How to break the pain barrier. The Times, 12 December: 12.

Holligan C. (1997) Theory in initial teacher education: students' perspectives on its utility – a case study. British Educational Research Journal 23, 4: 533–51.

Holmes BD, Mann KV, Hennen BKE (1990) Defining fitness and aptitude to practice medicine. Medical Teacher 12, 2: 181–91.

Holt J (1970) The Underachieving School. London: Pitman Publishing.

Howard C (1979) A Fair Assessment: Issues in Evaluating Coursework. London: Central Council for Education and Training in Social Work.

Hoyle E (1969) The Role of the Teacher. In Geary A (1998) Written judgements in school: a personal perspective. Early Child Development and Care 34, 241–65.

Hunter M, Barker G. (1987) If at first...attribution theory in classrooms. Education Leadership 45, 2: 50–3.

Hyland T (1991) Knowledge performance and competence-based assessment. EDUCA, December: 7.

Ilott I (1988) Failure: the Clinical Supervisor's Perspective. Unpublished MEd thesis, University of Nottingham.

Ilott I (1993) The process of failing occupational therapy students: a staff perspective. Unpublished PhD thesis, University of Nottingham.

Ilott I (1995) To fail or not to fail? A course for fieldwork educators. American Journal of Occupational Therapy 49, 3: 250–5.

Ilott I (1996) Ranking the problems of fieldwork supervision reveals a new problem: failing students. British Journal of Occupational Therapy 59, 11: 525–8.

Ilott I, Allen M (1997) Field testing the SHO core competencies and specialty specific competencies as pre-requisites for Higher Specialty Training. Report of a NHSE/DfEE Commissioned Project, Department of Postgraduate Medical and Dental Education, University of Leeds.

Irwin A (1995) Chemistry PhDs fail the acid test. The Times Higher Education Supplement, 7 April: 1.

JM Consulting Ltd (1996) The Regulation of Health Professions: Report of a Review of the Professions Supplementary to Medicine Act (1960) with recommendations for new legislation. Bristol: JM Consulting Ltd.

Jarvis P (1983) Adult and Continuing Education: Theory and Practice. London: Croom Helm.

Jenkins S (1996) In league with ignorance. The Times, 20 November: 20.

Jolly B, Wakeford R, Newble D (1994) Requirements for Action and Research in Certification and Recertification. In Newble D, Jolly B, Wakeford R (Eds) The

Certification and Recertification of Doctors: Issues in the Assessment of Clinical Competence. Cambridge: Cambridge University Press.

Kagan DM and Albertson LM (1987) Student teaching: perceptions of supervisory meetings. Journal of Education for Teaching 13, 1: 49–60.

Keys B, Henshall J (1990) Supervision: Concepts, Skills and Assessment. Chichester: John Wiley & Sons.

Kim A, Clifford MM (1988) Goal source, goal difficulty and individual difference variables as predictors of response to failure. British Journal of Educational Psychology 58: 28–43.

Koehler VR (1988) Teachers' beliefs about at–risk students. Paper presented at the Annual meeting of the American Educational Research Association.

Kremer-Hayon L. (1986) Supervisors' inner world: professional perspectives. European Journal of Teacher Education 9, 2: 181–7.

Kubler-Ross E (1969) On Death and Dying. New York: MacMillan.

Lankshear A. (1990) Failure to fail: the teacher's dilemma. Nursing Standard 4, 20: 35–7.

Law Report: December 12 1995 Professional misconduct in negligent treatment. The Times: 42.

Lawrence R (1985) School performance containment theory and delinquent behaviour. Youth and Society 17, 1: 69–95.

Leat DJK (1993) Competence, teaching, thinking and feelings. Oxford Review of Education 19, 4: 499–510.

Lengacher CA, Kelly R (1990) Academic predictors of success on the NCLEX–RN examination for associate degree nursing students. Journal of Nursing Education 29, 4: 163–9.

Lips HM (1991) Women, Men and Power. Toronto: Mayfield.

Low JF (1992) Another look at licensure: consumer protection or professional protectionism. American Journal of Occupational Therapy 46, 4: 373–6.

MacNeil M (1997) From nurse to teacher: recognising a status passage. Journal of Advanced Nursing 25: 634–42.

Majorowicz K (1986) Clinical grades and the grievance process. Nurse Educator 11, 2: 36–40.

Mashaba G, Mhlongo T (1995) Student nurse wastage: a case study of the profile and perceptions of students in an institution. Journal of Advanced Nursing 22: 364–73.

Maslach C (1982) Burnout – The Cost of Caring. New York: Prentice Hall.

Mcleod PJ, Harden RM (1985) Clinical teaching strategies for physicians. Medical Teacher 7, 2: 173–89.

Meisenhelder JB (1982) Clinical evaluation: an instructor's dilemma. Nursing Outlook, June: 348–51.

Mitchell L (1993) NVQs/SVQs at Higher Levels: A Discussion Paper to the Higher Levels Seminar. Competence and Assessment Briefing Series No. 8. Sheffield: Employment Department Group.

Murphy RJL (1989) The Role of External Examiners in Improving Student Assessments. In External Examining in Undergraduate Psychology Degrees. British Psychological Society, Occasional Paper No. 6.

Murphy RJL (1994) Dearing: a farewell to criterion referencing. British Journal of Curriculum and Assessment 4, 3: 10–12.

Murphy RJL (1995) Firsts among equals: the case of British university degrees. British Journal of Curriculum and Assessment 5, 2: 38–41, 45.

Murphy RJL (1996) Like a bridge over troubled water: realising the potential of educational research. British Educational Research Journal 22, 1: 3–15.

Murphy RJL (1997) Drawing outrageous conclusions from national assessment results: where will it all end? British Journal of Curriculum and Assessment, 2: 32–4.

Murphy RJL, Burke P, Gillespie J, Rainbow R, Wilmut J (1997) The Key Skills of Students Entering Higher Education. Report of a DfEE Commissioned Project, University of Nottingham.

Murphy RJL, Joyes G (1996) Marks and grades aren't necessarily evil. In Watson K (Ed.) Educational Dilemmas: Debates and Diversity. London: Cassell.

National Committee of Inquiry into Higher Education (1997) Higher Education in the Learning Society. Summary. The Times Higher Education Supplement, 25 July.

Nehring V (1990) Nursing clinical teacher effectiveness inventory: a replication study of the characteristics of 'best' and 'worst' clinical teachers as perceived by nursing faculty and students. Journal of Advanced Nursing 15: 934–40.

Newble D, Jolly B, Wakeford R (Eds) (1994) The Certification and Recertification of Doctors: Issues in the Assessment of Clinical Competence. Cambridge: Cambridge University Press.

Norcross L (1991) Ruthless policies may be needed. The Times, 29 July.

Nye M (1997) Look who's over here. The Times Higher Education Supplement HE Trends 1997. 26 September: iv.

Occupational Therapists Board (1996) Statement of Infamous Conduct. London: Council for the Professions Supplementary to Medicine.

O'Leary J (1997) Private schools' A levels wrongly upgraded. The Times, 10 January: 1.

O'Leary J, Webster P (1997) Teachers face sack if their pupils fail. The Times, 12 January: 1.

Partington J, Brown G, Gordon G (1993) Handbook for External Examiners in Higher Education. Sheffield: Committee of Vice–Chancellors and Principals of the Universities of the United Kingdom Universities' Staff Development Unit.

Paterson CF (1988) Annual survey of occupational therapy students: reasons for drop-out. British Journal of Occupational Therapy 51, 3: 81–3.

Pickis R (1993) CPSM and professional education registration and regulation. Paper presented at Council of Validation Universities' Workshop, University of Kent, 21 April.

Plewis I (1991) Underachievement: a case of conceptual confusion. British Educational Research Association 17, 4: 377–85.

Pollio HR, Eison JA, Milton O (1988) College grades as an adaptation level phenomenon. Contemporary Educational Psychology 13: 146–56.

Pollio HR, Humphreys WL, Eison JA (1991) Patterns of parental reaction. Higher Education 22: 31–42.

Pollio HR, Humphreys WL, Milton O (1989) Components of contemporary college grade meanings. Contemporary Educational Psychology 14: 77–91.

Pope LM (1983) State Regulation of Educator Evaluation. In Beckham J, Perry AZ (Eds) Legal Issues in Public Employment. Bloomington, Indiana: Phi Delta Kappa.

Poteet GW, Pollok CS (1981) When a student fails clinical. American Journal of Nursing, October: 1889–90.

Prawat RS, Byers JL, Anderson AH (1983) An attributional analysis of teachers' affective reaction to student success and failure. American Educational Review Journal 20, 2: 137–52.

Preston B (1993) One in ten primary teachers is 'inadequate'. The Times, 1 July.

Preston B (1995) Teachers underplay pupils' failings in jargon-filled reports. The Times, 7 August: 7.

Pyne RH (1981) Professional Discipline in Nursing: Theory and Practice. Oxford: Blackwell Scientific Publications.

Quality Assurance Agency for Higher Education (1998) Strengthening the external examiner system and developing the role of the registered external examiner. Higher Quality 1, 3: 15–18.

Raggatt P, Hevey D (1995) Sufficiency of Evidence: The Development of Guidance for Assessors and Verifiers. Research and Development Series Report 32. Sheffield: Department for Education and Employment's Learning Methods Branch.

Raviv A, Par-Tal D, Raviv A, Levit R (1983) Research symposium: attribution theory students' reactions to attributions of ability and effort. British Journal of Educational Psychology 53: 1–13.

Rittman MR, Osburn J (1995) An interpretative analysis of precepting an unsafe student. Journal of Nursing Education 34, 5: 217–21.

Rosenthal MM (1995) The Incompetent Doctor: Behind Closed Doors. Buckingham: Open University Press.

Rowntree D (1987) Assessing Students: How Shall we Know Them? London: Kogan Press.

Roy S (1996) Risk management. Nursing Standard 10, 18: 51–4.

Rozier CK, Gilkeson GE, Hamilton BL (1992) Why students choose occupational therapy as a career. American Journal of Occupational Therapy 46, 7: 626–32.

Scott C (1997) Relative Values. The Sunday Times Magazine, 23 November: 9–10.

Scott-Clark C (1996) Students with 0% can still get a degree. The Sunday Times, 7 July: 7.

Scott-Clark C, Hymas C (1996) Quarter of pupils have bad teachers. The Sunday Times, 28 January: 5.

Shah S, Cooper B (1992) Occupational therapy: a profession not a discipline. Australian Journal of Occupational Therapy 39, 4: 25–7.

Shepard LA, Smith ML (Eds) (1989) Flunking Grades: Research and Policies on Retention. Lewes: Falmer Press.

Shipley P (1990) Stress management: palliative or preventive. Occupational Health Review, June/July: 24–5.

Shtogren JA (1980) The Structure of Competence – The Theories and Facts about Managing People. Bromley: Chartwell-Bratt.

Silver H (1993) External Examiners: Changing Roles? London: Council for National Academic Awards.

Slapper G (1996) Bad marks or bad marking? The Times, 8 October: 39.

Smith R (1997) All doctors are problem doctors. British Medical Journal 314: 481–2.

Smyth WJ (Ed.) (1986) Learning about Teaching Through Clinical Supervision. London: Croom Helm.

Snyder CR, Higgins RL (1988) Excuses: their effective role in the negotiation of reality. Psychological Bulletin 104, 1: 23–35.

Stabile RG (1989) Whose fault is student failure? American School Board Journal January: 28–9.

Stacey M (1995) Medical Accountability. In Hunt G (Ed.) Whistleblowing in the Health Service. London: Edward Arnold.

Stephenson J (1994) Opinion: Capability and competence. Are they the same and does it matter? Capability 1, 1: 3–4.

Stevens R, Pihl RO (1987) Seventh grade students at–risk for school failure. Adolescence 12, 86: 333–45.

Stewart AM (1980) The study of occupational therapy teaching resources in the United Kingdom. British Journal of Occupational Therapy, January: 3–6.

Stewart V, Stewart A (1982) Managing the Poor Performer. Aldershot: Gower.

Stone HL (1982) Return to 'basics' in medical education: a commentary. Medical Teacher 4, 3: 102–3.

Strauss RP, Sawyer AE (1986) Some new evidence on teacher and student competencies. Economics of Education Review 5, 1: 41–8.

Streifer PA (1987) Teacher Evaluation Systems: A Review of Critical Issues and the Current State of the Art. Andover, Massachusetts: The Regional Laboratory.

Sutherland S (1998) Personal view: senates face emasculation. The Times Higher Education Supplement, 3 April: 11.

Symanski ME (1991) Reducing the effect of faculty demoralisation when failing students. Nurse Educator 16, 3: 18–22.

The Times Higher Education Supplement (1996) The natives are restive – Opinion. 12 July: 9.

Tollefson N, Chen JS (1988) Consequences of teachers' attributions for student failure. Teaching and Teacher Education 4, 3: 259–65.

Towle C (1954) The Learner in Education for the Professions: As Seen in the Education for Social Work. Chicago, Illinois: University of Chicago Press.

Travers A (1982) Ritual power in interaction. Symbolic Interaction 5, 2: 277–86.

Turkett S (1987) Let's take the 'i' out of failure. Journal of Nursing Education 26, 2: 246–7.

Turner B (1996) A test of my nerves and finances as much as my offspring's wisdom. The Times. 15 August: 9.

Tysome T (1994) Cheating purge: inspectors out. The Times Higher Education Supplement August 19th: 1.

Tytler D (1995) On your marks for the results season. The Times. 14 August: 33.

Ungerleider D (1985) Uncontrolled rage: an overlooked cause of remediation failure. Paper presented at the International Conference of the Association for Children and Adults with Learning Disabilities.

United Kingdom Central Council for Nursing Midwifery and Health Visiting (1994) Professional Conduct – Occasional Report on Standards of Nursing in Nursing Homes. London: UKCC.

Utley A (1997) Anglia may face legal action. The Times Higher Education Supplement, 21 March: 2.

Vincent C (1995) Editorial: Clinical risk management: one piece of the quality jigsaw. Quality in Health Care 4: 73–4.

Warren-Piper D (1994) Are Professors Professional? The Organisation of University Examinations. London: Jessica Kingsley Publishers.

Westcott E. (1995) Budget against student wastage. The Times Higher Education Supplement, 6 October: 14.

White J (1989) Student teaching as a rite of passage. Anthropology and Education Quarterly 20: 177–95.

Wilder G (1997) Compensation claims: pay–back time. Health Services Journal, 20 March: 28–31.

Wiliam D, Black P (1996) Meanings and consequences: a basis for distinguishing formative and summative functions of assessment? British Educational Research Journal 22, 5: 537–48.

Wilson J (1996) An introduction to risk management in the primary sector. British Journal of Health Care Management 2, 1: 34–6.

Wilson JD (1972) Student failures. Educational Review 25, 1: 21–33.

Wojtas O (1995) A sparkling career. The Times Higher Education Supplement, 17 March: 23.

Wolf A, Silver R (1995) Measuring 'Broad' Skills: Issues for Assessment. Research and Development Series Report 31. Sheffield: Department for Education and Employment's Learning Methods Branch.

Wong J (1979) The inability to transfer classroom learning to clinical nursing practice. Journal of Advanced Nursing 4: 161–8.

Wong J, Wong S (1987) Towards effective clinical teaching in nursing. Journal of Advanced Nursing 12: 505–12.

Wood V, Campbell DB (1985) The instructor the student and appeals. Nurse Education Today 5: 241–6.

Woodyard J, Darby MA (1996) Complaints: vicious circles. Health Service Journal, 26 September: 30–1.

Worth-Butler M, Fraser D, Murphy RJL (1995) The need to define competence in midwifery. British Journal of Midwifery 3, 5: 259–62.

Wright P. (1996) Degrees in a class of their own. The Times Higher Education Supplement, 5 July: 10–11.

Yalom ID (1985) The Theory and Practice of Group Psychotherapy. New York: Basic Books.

Yerxa EJ (1983) Audacious values: the energy source of occupational therapy. In Kielhofner G (Ed.) Health Through Occupation: Theory and Practice in Occupational Therapy. Philadelphia, Pennsylvania: FA Davies.

Yerxa EJ (1986) Problems of evaluating fieldwork students. In Guide to Fieldwork Education. Bethesda, Maryland: American Occupational Therapy Association.

Index